Jekka's
CULINARY HERBS

Jekka's CULINARY HERBS

JEKKA McVICAR

KYLE CATHIE LIMITED

To Mum

First published as *Jekka's Culinary Herbs*
in Great Britain in 1995 by
Kyle Cathie Limited
20 Vauxhall Bridge Road, London SW1V 2SA

This edition published 1995

ISBN 1 85626 207 3

2 4 6 8 10 9 7 5 3 1

The material in this book is taken from
Jekka's Complete Herb Book

Photographs © Jessica McVicar 1994
© Michelle Garrett 1994 © Sally Maltby 1994

Artwork © Sally Maltby 1994

Book design by Geoff Hayes
Cover design by Tom Murdoch and Geoff Hayes

Printed and bound in Spain
by Graficas Reunidas, S.A., Madrid.

Jessica McVicar is hereby identified as the author of this
work in accordance with Section 77 of the Copyright,
Designs and Patents Act, 1988.

A Cataloguing in Publication record for this title is available
from the British Library.

Acknowledgements
With many thanks to Mac for all his support, Anthea for
turning up in the nick of time, Kyle for taking the gamble,
Piers for all his reading and Penny for her compliments.

Photographic acknowledgements
Plant photography by Jekka McVicar and Sally Maltby.
All other photography by Michelle Garrett.

CONTENTS

INTRODUCTION

Hippocrates said 'Let your medicine be your food, and your food your medicine.'

Herbs have been used since man has been on Earth as a food and a medicine. There are few plants capable of providing the sheer pleasure of herbs; they are the most generous of plants, aromatic and attractive, useful in both the home and the garden, health-giving and healthy.

The increasing interest in herbs is part of a movement towards a healthier lifestyle, symbolising a more natural approach. Herbs are used in cooking, in domestic products, alternative medicines and cosmetics; and they affect the quality of life in many ways.

The most extraordinary feature of herbs is their incredible versatility. You may think of a particular herb as having mainly culinary or medicinal properties and then discover it has other useful applications. Thyme for example, provides the raw material for cooking, medicines and aromatherapy.

What is a herb? It can be argued that all useful plants are herbs. The Oxford English Dictionary defines them as 'Plants of which the leaves, stem or flowers are used for food or medicine, or in some way for their scent or flavour'. To elaborate, a herb can be any plant used as an ingredient in food or drink for flavour or preservative properties, in medicine for health-giving properties, or in perfume, cosmetics or aromatherapy as a fixative, for flavour or aroma or as a cleansing agent. That herbs do you good is in no doubt, improving your health, appearance or sense of well-being.

Growing ones own culinary herbs, either in the garden or in a container, will add another dimension to the kitchen. The aroma when you cook with them will wet the appetite and the flavour when you eat them will transform your taste buds. Until recently cooks have had a limited range of fresh herbs to choose from; however with the increasing interest in herbs every year there are new introductions from afar to tempt us to try new recipes. Herbs used in cooking are a definite must for the health conscious cooks, they are packed with minerals and vitamins, any which have a peppermint flavour or aniseed flavour aid digestion, others stimulate the appetite, or lower the cholesterol, and they are a bonus for those on a low salt diet. Not only do they do all this but, as the Romans discovered, they are in their own rights great food preservatives. Another point worth remembering is that it is not just the leaf of the herb that is edible, in the case of Chives and Salad Rocket, the flowers are delicious, and the seeds from Dill, Coriander, Lovage and Fennel are of equal importance as the leaf in many culinary dishes. Whether you cook with herbs or eat them raw in salads, I advise you start slowly and build your taste buds up. Some of the flavours like savory can be very strong. I totally endorse a quote from my Grandmother (Ruth Lowinsky) book 'Food for Pleasure'. 'Use herbs assiduously; yes, but not in large quantities. Herbs have been necessary in good cooking for hundreds of years. This does not mean that, when they cover the flavour of the main ingredient, the dish is more palatable. They should enhance the flavour of fish or meat not overwhelm it.'

When planning a herb garden there are no restrictions on how it should be laid out, formally or informally, as a border, or in a pot. The only factors you must consider are: what are the soil conditions like? How sunny or shady is the area you have chosen? Would this suit the herbs you want to plant? If you find the area unsuitable for a particular herb and you have no wish to re-design your garden, plant them in containers as you will find that most herbs are accommodating plants and will grow happily in them as long as you take due consideration of their pot size. This then frees you to place them in the position that most suits them and your design. If necessary sinking the pots into the ground to disguise them. Bearing in mind that this is a culinary herb garden I do advise you to place the plants near the kitchen or front door, if this is more convenient, because if you have them planted at the bottom of the vegetable garden and it is pouring with rain there will be no chance of you running out to pick a sprig of tarragon or thyme. Finally I must stress that all herbs grown for either culinary or medicinal use should, without any excuses, be grown free from the use of chemicals.

Jekka McVicar

PROPAGATION

One of the great joys of gardening is propagating your own plants. Success is dependent on adequate preparation and the care and attention you give during the critical first few weeks. The principles remain the same, but techniques are constantly changing. There is always something new to discover.

The three main methods of propagating new plants are by Seed, Cuttings and Layering.

This chapter provides general, step-by-step instructions for each of these methods. As there are always exceptions to a rule, please refer to the propagation section under each individual herb.

SEED

Sowing Outside

Most annual herbs grow happily propagated year after year from seed sown directly into the garden. There are two herbs worth mentioning where that is not the case – sweet marjoram, because the seed is so small it is better started in a pot; and basil because, in damp northern climates like that in Britain, the young seedlings will rot off.

In an average season the seed should be sown in mid- to late spring after the soil has been prepared and warmed. Use the arrival of weed seedlings in the garden as a sign that the temperature is rising. Herbs will survive in a range of different soils. Most culinary herbs originate from the Mediterranean so their preference is for a sandy free-draining soil. If your soil is sticky clay do not give up, give the seeds a better start by adding a fine layer of horticultural sand along the drill when preparing the seed bed.

Preparation of Seed Bed

Before starting, check your soil type making sure that the soil has sufficient food to maintain a seed bed. Dig the bed over, mark out a straight line with a piece of string secured tightly over each row, draw a shallow drill, 6-13mm (¼/½in) deep, using the side of a fork or hoe, and sow the seeds thinly, 2 or 3 per 25mm (1in). Do not overcrowd the bed, otherwise the seedlings will grow leggy and weak and be prone to disease.

Protected Sowing

Starting off the seeds in a greenhouse or on a windowsill gives you more control over the warmth and moisture they need, and enables you to begin propagating earlier in the season.

Nothing is more uplifting than going into the greenhouse on a cold and gloomy late-winter morning and seeing all the seedlings emerging. It makes one enthusiastic for spring.

Preparation of Seed

Most seeds need air, light, temperature and moisture to germinate. Some have a long dormancy, and some have hard outer coats and need a little help to get going. Here are two techniques.

Scarification
If left to nature, seeds that have a hard outer coat would take a long time to germinate. To speed up the process, rub the seed between 2 sheets of fine sandpaper. This weakens the coat of the seed so that moisture essential for germination can penetrate.

Stratification (vernalization)
Some seeds need a period of cold (from 1 to 6 months) to germinate. Mix the seed with damp sand and place in a plastic bag in the refrigerator or freezer. After 4 weeks sow on the surface of the compost and cover with Perlite. My family always enjoys this time of year. They go to the freezer to get the ice cream and find herb seed instead.

Preparation of Seed Container

One of the chief causes of diseased compost is a dirty propagation container. To minimize the spread of disease, remove any 'tidemarks' of compost, soil or chemicals around the insides of the pots and seed trays. Wash and scrub them thoroughly with washing up liquid, rinse with water and give a final rinse with diluted Jeyes fluid. Leave for 24 hours before re-use. Old compost also provides ideal conditions for damping off fungi and sciarid flies. To avoid cross-infection always remove spent compost from the greenhouse or potting shed.

Compost

It is always best to use a sterile seed compost. Ordinary garden soil contains many weed seeds that could easily be confused with the germinating herb seed. The compost used for most seed sowing is 50per cent propagating bark and 50per cent peat-based seed compost and unless stated otherwise within the specific herb section, this is the mix to use. However, for herbs that

Misting Unit

prefer a freer draining compost, or for those that require stratification outside, I advise using a 25 per cent peat-based seed compost: 50 per cent propagating bark and 25 per cent horticultural grit mix. And if you are sowing seeds that have a long germination period, use a soil-based seed compost.

Sowing in Seed Trays
Preparation: fill a clean seed tray with compost up to 1cm (½in) below the rim and firm down with a flat piece of wood. Do not to press too hard as this will over-compress the compost and restrict drainage, encouraging damping off disease and attack by sciarid fly.

The gap below the rim is essential, as it prevents the surface sown seeds and compost being washed over the edge when watering, and it allows room for growth when you are growing under card or glass.

Water the prepared tray using a fine rose on the watering can. Do not over-water. The compost should be damp, not soaking. After an initial watering, water as little as possible, but never let the surface dry out. Once the seed is sown lack of moisture can prevent germination and kill the seedlings, but too much water excludes oxygen and encourages damping-off fungi and root rot. Be sure to use a fine rose on the watering can so as not to disturb the seed.

Sowing Methods
There are 3 main methods, the choice dependent on the size of the seed. They are, in order of seed size, fine to large:

1 Scatter on the surface of the compost, and cover with a fine layer of Perlite.

2 Press into the surface of the compost, either with your hand or a flat piece of wood the size of the tray,

and cover with Perlite.
3 Press down to 1 seed's depth and cover with compost.

The Cardboard Trick
When seeds are too small to handle, you can control distribution by using a thin piece of card (cereal cartons are good), cut to 10cm x 5cm (4in x 2in), and folded down the middle. Place a small amount of seed into the folded card and gently tap it over the prepared seed tray. This technique is especially useful when sowing into plug trays (see below).

Sowing in Plug (Module) Trays (Multi-cell Trays)
These plug trays are a great invention. The seed can germinate in its own space, get established into a strong seedling, and make a good root ball. When potting on, the young plant remains undisturbed and will continue growing, rather than coming to a halt because it has to regenerate roots to replace those damaged in pricking out from the seed tray. This is very good for plants like coriander, which hate being transplanted and tend to bolt if you move them. Another advantage is that as you are sowing into individual cells, the problem of overcrowding is cut to a minimum, and damping-off disease and sciarid fly are easier to control. Also, because seedlings in plugs are easier to maintain, planting out or potting on is not so critical.

Plug trays come in different sizes; for example, you can get trays with very small holes of 15mm (½in) x

15mm up to trays with holes of 36.5mm (1¼in) x 36.5mm. To enable a reasonable time lapse between germination and potting on, I recommend the larger.

When preparing these trays for seed sowing, make sure you have enough space, otherwise compost seems to land up everywhere. Prepare the compost and fill the tray right to the top, scraping off surplus compost with a piece of wood level with the top of the holes. It is better not to firm the compost down. Watering in (see above) settles the compost enough to allow space for the seed and the top dressing of Perlite. For the gardener-in-a-hurry there are available in good garden centres ready-prepared propagation trays, which are plug trays already filled with compost. All you have to do is water and add the seed.

The principles of sowing in plug trays are the same as for trays. Having sown your seed, DO label the trays clearly with the name of the plant, and also the date. The date is useful as one can check their late or speedy germination. It is also good for record keeping, if you want to sow them again next year, and helps with organizing the potting on.

Seed Germination
Seeds need warmth and moisture to germinate.

The main seed sowing times are autumn and spring. This section provides general information with the table below providing a quick look guide to germination. Any detailed advice specific to a particular herb is provided in the A-Z Herb section.

Quick Germination Guide
Hot 27-32°C (80-90°F)
Rosemary

Warm 15-21°C (60-70°F)
Most plants, including those from the Mediterranean, and Chives and Parsley.

Cool 4-10°C (40-50°F)
Lavenders. (Old lavender seed will need a period of stratification).

Stratification
Arnica (old seed), Sweet Woodruff, Yellow Iris, Poppy, Soapwort, Sweet Cicely, Hops (old seed), Sweet Violet.

Scarification
All leguminous species, i.e., broom, trefoils, clovers and vetches.

Need Light (i.e., do not cover)
Chamomile, Foxglove, Thyme, Winter Savory, Poppy and Sweet Marjoram.

In a cold greenhouse, a heated propagator may be needed in early spring for herbs that germinate at warm to hot temperatures. In the house you can use a shelf near a radiator (never on the radiator), or an airing cupboard. Darkness does not hinder the germination of most herbs (see table above for exceptions), but if you put your containers in an airing cupboard YOU MUST CHECK THEM EVERY DAY. As soon as there is any sign of life, place the trays in a warm light place, but not in direct sunlight.

Hardening Off
When large enough to handle, prick out seed tray seedlings and pot up individually. Allow them to root fully.

Test plug tray seedlings by giving one or two a gentle tug. They should come away from the cells cleanly, with the root ball. If they do not, leave for another few days.

When the seedlings are ready, harden them off gradually by leaving the young plants outside during the day. Once weaned into a natural climate, either plant them directly into a prepared site in the garden, or into a larger container for the summer.

CUTTINGS

Taking cuttings is sometimes the only way to propagate (e.g. non-flowering herbs, such as **Chamomile Treneague**, and variegated forms, such as Tri-color Sage).

It is not as difficult as some people suggest, and even now I marvel at how a mere twig can produce roots and start the whole life cycle going again.

There are 4 types of cutting used in herb growing:

1 Softwood cuttings taken in spring

2 Semi-hardwood cuttings taken in summer

3 Hardwood cuttings taken in autumn

4 Root cuttings, which can be taken in spring and autumn.

For successful softwood cuttings it is worth investing in a heated propagator, which can be placed either in a greenhouse or on a shady windowsill. For success-ful semi-ripe, hardwood and root cuttings, a shaded cold frame can be used.

Softwood Cuttings
Softwood cuttings are taken from the new lush green growth of most perennial herbs between spring and mid-summer, a few examples being Balm of Gilead, Bergamot, the Chamomiles, the Mints, Prostanthera, the Rosemarys, the Scented Geraniums, the Thymes, Curly Wood Sage and Wormwood. Check under the individual herb entries in the A-Z section for more specific information.

1 The best way to get a plant to produce successful rooting material is to prune it vigorously in winter (which will encourage rapid growth when the temperature rises in the spring), and to take cuttings as soon as there is sufficient growth.

2 Fill a pot, seed tray, or plug tray with cutting compost – 50 per cent bark, 50 per cent peat. It is important to use a well-draining medium rather than standard potting mixes as, without root systems, cuttings are prone to wet rot.

Firm the compost to within 2cm (¾in) of the rim.

If space is limited or pots are unavailable, you can pack the base of several cuttings in damp sphagnum moss (rolled up firmly in a polythene strip and held in place by a rubber band or string) until the roots form.

3 Collect the cuttings in small batches in the morning. Choose sturdy shoots with plenty of leaves. Best results come from non-flowering shoots with the base leaves removed. Cut the shoot with a knife, not scissors. This is because scissors tend to pinch or seal the end of the cutting thus hindering rooting.

4 Place the cutting at once in the shade in a polythene bag or a bucket of water. Softwood cuttings are extremely susceptible to water loss; even a small loss will hinder root development. If the cuttings cannot be dealt with quickly, keep them in the cool (e.g. in a salad box from a refrigerator) to prevent excessive water loss.

5 To prepare the cutting material, cut the base of the stem 5mm (¼in) below a leaf joint, to leave a cutting of roughly 10cm (4in) long.

6 If the cutting material has to be under 10cm (4in), take the cutting with a heel. Remove the lower leaves and trim the tail which is left from the heel.

7 Trim the stem cleanly before a node, the point at which a leaf stalk joins the stem. Remove the leaves from the bottom third of the cutting, leaving at least 2 or 3 leaves on top. The reason for leaving leaves on cuttings is that the plant feeds through them as it sets root. Do not tear off the base leaves as this can cause disease; use a knife and gently cut them off.

8 Make a hole with a dibber in the compost and insert the cutting up to its leaves. Make sure that the leaves do not touch or go below the surface of the compost; they will rot away and may cause a fungus condition which can spread up the stem and to other cuttings. Do not overcrowd the container or include more than one species, because quite often they take different times to root. (For instance, keep box and thymes separate.)

Hormone rooting-powders that some gardeners use, contain synthetic plant hormones and fungicide and are not for the organic grower; following my detailed instructions you should find them unnecessary. However, they may help with difficult cuttings. The cutting should be dipped into the rooting-powder just before inserting into the compost.

9 Label and date the cuttings clearly, and only water the compost from above if necessary (the initial watering after preparing the container should be sufficient). Keep out of direct sunlight in hot weather. In fact, if it is very sunny, heavy shade is best for the first week.

Either place in a heated or unheated propagator, or cover the pot or container with a plastic bag supported on a thin wire hoop (to prevent the plastic touching the leaves), or with an upturned plastic bottle with the bottom cut off. If you are using a plastic bag, make sure you turn it inside out every few days to stop excess moisture from condensation dropping onto the cuttings.

10 Spray the cuttings every day with water for the first week. Do this in the morning, never at night. Do not test for rooting too early by tugging the cutting up, as you may disturb it at a crucial time. A better way to check for new roots is to look underneath the container. Average rooting time is 2-4 weeks.

The cutting medium is low in nutrients, so give a regular foliar feed when the cutting starts to root.

11 Harden off the cuttings gradually when they are rooted. Bring them out in stages to normal sunny, airy conditions.

12 Pot them on using a prepared potting compost once they are weaned. Label and water well after transplanting.

13 About 4-5 weeks after transplanting, when you can see that the plant is growing away, pinch out the top centre of the young cutting. This will encourage the plant to bush out, making it stronger as well as fuller.

14 Allow to grow on until a good-size root ball can be seen in the pot – check occasionally by gently removing the plant from the pot – then plant out.

Semi-hardwood Cuttings or Greenwood Cuttings
Usually taken from shrubby herbs such as Rosemary and Myrtle towards the end of the growing season (from mid-summer to mid-autumn). Use the same method (steps 2-8) as for softwood cuttings, with the following exceptions:

2 The compost should be freer-draining than for softwood cuttings, as semi-hardwood cuttings will be left for longer (see 10 below). Make the mix equal parts peat, grit and bark.

9 Follow step 9 for softwood cuttings, but place the pot, seed tray or plug tray in a cold greenhouse, cold frame, cool conservatory, or on a cold windowsill in a garage, not in a propagator, unless it has a misting unit.

10 Average rooting time for semi-hardwood cuttings is 4-6 weeks. Follow step 10 except for the watering schedule. Instead, if the autumn is exceptionally hot and the compost or cuttings seem to be drying out, spray once a week. Again, do this in the morning, and be careful not to over-water.

11 Begin the hardening off process in the spring after the frosts. Give a foliar feed as soon as there is sufficient new growth.

Hardwood Cuttings
Taken mid- to late autumn in exactly the same way as softwood cuttings steps 2-8, but with a freer draining compost of equal parts peat, grit and bark. Keep watering to the absolute minimum. Winter in a cold frame, greenhouse or conservatory. Average rooting time can take as long as 12 months.

Root Cuttings
This method of cutting is suitable for plants with creeping roots, such as Bergamot, Comfrey, Horseradish, Lemon Balm, Mint. Soapwort and Sweet Woodruff.

1 Dig up some healthy roots in spring or autumn.

2 Fill a pot, seed tray or plug tray with cutting compost – 50 per cent bark, 50 per cent peat, firmed to within 3cm (1in) of the rim. Water well and leave to stand while preparing your cutting material.

3 Cut 4-8cm (1.5-3in) lengths of root that carry a

growing bud. It is easy to see the growing buds on the roots of mint.

This method is equally applicable for all the varieties mentioned above as suitable for root propagation, with the exception of Comfrey and Horseradish, where one simply slices the root into sections, 4-8cm (1½-3in) long, using a sharp knife to give a clean cut through the root. Do not worry, each will produce a plant!
These cuttings lend themselves to being grown in plug trays.

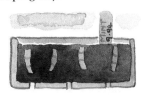

4 Make holes in the compost with a dibber. If using pots or seed trays these should be 3-6cm (1-2½in) apart. Plant the cutting vertically.

5 Cover the container with a small amount of compost, followed by a layer of Perlite level with the top of the container.

6 Label and date. This is most important because you cannot see what is in the container until the plant begins to grow and it is all too easy to forget what you have planted.

7 Average rooting time 2-3 weeks. Do not water until roots or top growth appears. Then apply liquid feed.

8 Slowly harden off the cuttings when rooted.

9 Pot on in a potting

compost once they are weaned. Label and water well after transplanting. You can miss this stage out if you have grown the root cuttings in plug trays.

10 About 2-3 weeks after transplanting, when you can see that the plant is growing away, pinch out the top centre of the young cutting. This will encourage the plant to bush out, making it stronger as well as fuller.

11 Allow to grow on until a good-size root ball can be seen in the pot. Plant out in the garden when the last frosts are over.

LAYERING

If cuttings are difficult to root you can try layering, a process that encourages sections of plant to root while still attached to the parent. Bay, Rosemary, Sage are good examples of plants that suit this method.

1 Prune some low branches off the parent plant during the winter season to induce vigorous growth and cultivate the soil around the plant during winter and early spring by adding peat and grit to it.

2 Trim the leaves and side shoots of a young vigorous stem for 10-60cm (4-24in) below its growing tip.

3 Bring the stem down to ground level and mark its position on the soil. Dig a trench at that point, making one vertical side 10-15cm (4-6in) deep, and the other sloping towards the plant.

4 Roughen the stem at the point where it will touch the ground.

5 Peg it down into the trench against the straight side, then bend the stem at right angles behind the growing tip, so that it protrudes vertically. Then

return the soil to the trench to bury the stem. Firm in well.

6 Water well using a watering can and keep the soil moist, especially in dry periods.

7 Sever the layering stem from its parent plant in autumn if well rooted, and 3-4 weeks later nip out the growing tip from the rooted layer to make plant bush out.

8 Check carefully that the roots have become well established before lifting the layered stem. If necessary, leave for a further year.

9 Replant either in the open ground or in a pot using the bark, grit, peat mix of compost. Label and leave to establish.

Mound Layering
A method similar to layering that not only creates new growth but also improves the appearance of old plants. This is particularly suitable for sages and thymes, which can woody in the centre.

1 In the spring, pile soil mixed with peat and sand over the bare woody centre until only young shoots show.

2 By late summer, roots will have formed on many of these shoots. They can be taken and planted in new locations as cuttings or by root division.

3 The old plant can then be dug up and disposed of.

HERB OILS, VINEGARS AND PRESERVES

Many herbs have antiseptic and anti-bacterial qualities, and were used in preserving long before there were cookbooks. Herbs aid digestion, stimulate appetite and enhance the flavour of food. I hope the following recipes will tempt you, because a variety of herb oils and vinegars can lead to the creation of unusual and interesting dishes. Herbs can make salad dressings, tomato-based sauces for pasta dishes, marinades for fish and meat, and can act as softening agents for vegetables, introducing a miriad of new tastes and flavours. They also make marvellous presents.

HERB OILS

These can be used in salad dressings, in marinades, sauces, stir-fry dishes and sautéing. Find some interesting bottles with good shapes. To start with, you need a clean glass jar, large enough to hold 500ml/¾pint/2cups with a screw top.

Basil oil

This is one of the best ways of storing and capturing the unique flavour of basil.

4 tablespoons/⅓cup basil leaves
500ml/¾pint/2cups olive or sunflower oil

Pick over the basil, remove the leaves from the stalks, and crush them in a mortar. For Greek basil, with its small leaves, simply crush in the mortar. Pound very slightly. Add a little oil and pound gently again. This bruises the leaves, so releasing their own oil into the oil. Mix the leaves with the rest of the oil and pour into a wide-necked jar and seal tightly. Place the jar on a sunny windowsill. Shake it every other day; and, after 2 weeks, strain through muslin into a decorative bottle and add a couple of fresh leaves of the relevant basil. This helps to identify the type of basil used and also looks fresh and enticing. Label. Adapt for dill, fennel (green), sweet marjoram, rosemary and garden or lemon thyme.

Garlic makes a very good oil. Use 4 cloves of garlic, peeled and crushed, and combined with the oil.

Bouquet garni oil

I use this oil for numerous dishes.

1 tablespoon sage
1 tablespoon lemon thyme
1 tablespoon Greek oregano
1 tablespoon French parsley
1 bay leaf
500ml/¾pint/2cups olive or sunflower oil

Break all the leaves and mix them together in a mortar, pounding lightly. Add a small amount of the oil to mix well, allowing the flavours to infuse. Pour into a wide-necked jar with the remaining oil. Cover and leave on a sunny windowsill for 2–3 weeks. Either shake or stir the jar every other day. Strain through muslin into an attractive bottle. If there is room, add a fresh sprig of each herb used.

SWEET OILS

Good with fruit dishes, marinades and puddings. Use almond oil, which combines well with scented flowers such as pinks, lavender, lemon verbena, rose petals and scented geraniums. Make as for savoury oils above. Mix 4 tablespoons of torn petals or leaves with 500ml/¾pint/2cups almond oil.

SPICE OILS

Ideal for salad dressings, they can be used for sautéing and stir-frying too. The most suitable herb spices are: coriander seeds, dill seeds and fennel seeds. Combine 2 tablespoons of seeds with 500ml/¾pint/2cups olive or sunflower oil, having first pounded the seeds gently to crush them in a mortar and mixed them with a little of the oil. Add a few of the whole seeds to the oil before bottling and labelling. Treat as for savoury oils and store.

HERBAL VINEGARS

Made in much the same way as oils, they can be used in gravies and sauces, marinades and salad dressings.

10 tablespoons chopped herb, such as basil, chervil, dill, fennel, garlic, lemon balm, marjoram, mint, rosemary, savory, tarragon or thyme
500ml/¾pint/2cups white wine or cider vinegar

Pound the leaves gently in a mortar. Heat half the vinegar until warm but not boiling, and pour it over the herbs in the mortar. Pound further to release the flavours of the herb. Leave to cool. Mix this mixture with the remaining vinegar and pour into a wide-necked bottle. Seal tightly. Remember to use an acid-proof lid (lining the existing lid with greaseproof paper is a way round this). Put on a sunny windowsill and shake each day for 2 weeks. Test for flavour; if a stronger taste is required, strain the vinegar and repeat with fresh herbs. Store as is or strain through double muslin and rebottle. Add a fresh sprig of the chosen herb to the bottle for ease of identification.

To Save Time

1 bottle white wine vinegar (500ml/¾pint/2cups)
4 large sprigs herb
4 garlic cloves, peeled

Pour off a little vinegar from the bottle and push in 2 sprigs of herb and the garlic cloves. Top up with the reserved vinegar if necessary. Reseal the bottle and leave on a sunny windowsill for 2 weeks. Change the herb sprigs for fresh ones and the vinegar is now ready to use.

Seed vinegar

Make as for herb vinegar, but the amounts used are

2 tablespoons of seeds to 600ml/1pint/2½cups white wine or cider vinegar. Seeds that make well-flavoured vinegars include dill, fennel and coriander.

Floral vinegar
Made in the same way, these are used for fruit salads and cosmetic recipes. Combine elder, nasturtiums, sweet violets, pinks, lavender, primrose, rose petals, rosemary or thyme flowers in the following proportions:

10 tablespoons torn flower heads or petals
500ml/¾pint/2cups white wine vinegar

Pickled horseradish
As a child I lived in a small village in the West of England where an old man called Mr Bell sat outside his cottage crying in the early autumn. It took me a long time to understand why – he was scraping the horseradish root into a bowl to make pickle. He did this outside because the fumes given off by the horseradish were so strong they made one's eyes water.

Wash and scrape the skin off a good size horseradish root. Mince in a food processor or grate it (if you can stand it!). Pack into small jars and cover with salted vinegar made from 1 teaspoon salt to ½pint cider or white wine vinegar. Seal and leave for 4 weeks before using.

Pickled nasturtium seeds
Poor man's capers! Pick nasturtium seeds while still green. Steep in brine made from 100g/4oz salt to 1litre/1¾pints water for 24 hours. Strain the seeds and put 2 tablespoons of seeds into a small jar. Add l clove of peeled garlic, 1 teaspoon black peppercorns, 1 teaspoon dill seeds and 1 tablespoon English mace leaves and fill with white wine vinegar, heated to simmering point. Strain and pour over the seeds. Seal the jars with acid-proof lids and leave for about 4 weeks. After opening, store in the refrigerator, and use the contents quickly.

SAVOURY HERB JELLY
Use the following herbs: sweet marjoram, mints (all kinds), rosemary, sage, summer savory, tarragon and common thyme.
Makes 2 x 350g/12oz jars

1kg/2lb tart cooking apples or crab apples, roughly chopped, cores and all
900ml/1½pints/3¾cups water
500g/1lb/2cups sugar
2 tablespoons wine vinegar
2 tablespoons lemon juice
1 bunch herbs, approx 15g/½oz
4 tablespoons chopped herbs

Put the apples into a large pan with the bunch of herbs and cover with cold water in a preserving pan. Bring to the boil and simmer until the apples are soft, roughly 30 minutes. Pour into a jelly bag and drain overnight.

Measure the strained juice and add 500g/1lb sugar to every 600ml/1pint fluid. Stir over gentle heat until the sugar has dissolved. Bring to the boil, stirring, and boil until setting point is reached. This takes roughly 20–30 minutes. Skim the surface scum and stir in the vinegar and lemon juice and the chopped herbs. Pour into jars, seal and label before storing.

SWEET JELLIES
Follow the above recipe, omitting the vinegar and lemon juice, and instead adding 150ml/¼pint/1cup water. The following make interestingly flavoured sweet jellies: bergamot, lavender flower, lemon verbena, scented geranium, sweet violet and lemon balm.

PRESERVES

Coriander chutney
Makes 2 x 500g/1lb jars

1kg/2lb cooking apples, peeled, cored and sliced
500g/1lb onions, peeled and roughly chopped
2 cloves garlic, peeled and crushed
1 red and 1 green pepper, deseeded and sliced
900ml/1½pints/3¾cups red wine vinegar
500g/1lb soft brown sugar
½ tablespoon whole coriander seeds
6 peppercorns tied securely in a piece of muslin
6 all-spice berries
50g/2oz root ginger, peeled and sliced
2 tablespoons coriander leaves, chopped
2 tablespoons mint, chopped

Combine the apples with the onions, garlic and peppers in a large, heavy saucepan. Add the vinegar and bring to the boil, simmering for about 30 minutes until all the ingredients are soft. Add the brown sugar and the muslin bag of seeds and berries. Then add the ginger. Heat, gently stirring all the time, until the sugar has dissolved, and simmer until thick; this can take up to 60 minutes. Stir in the chopped coriander and mint and spoon into hot, sterilized jars. Seal and label when cool.

Basil oil, coriander seed vinegar and coriander oil all make delicious additions to the store cupboard

SALAD HERB GARDEN

Herbs in salads make the difference between boring and interesting; they add flavour, texture and colour (especially the flowers).

Included in the design is a selection of Salad Herbs and Salad Herb Flowers. There are two tall herbs in the middle, chicory and red orach (blue and red), which are planted opposite each other. Also, I have positioned the only other tall plant – borage – on the outside ring, opposite the chicory so that the blue flowers together will make a vivid splash. To make access easy, there is an inner ring of stepping stones.

The herbs chosen are my choice and can easily be changed if you want to include a particular favourite. Remember to look at the heights; for instance, do not plant angelica in the outside circle because it will hide anything in the inner circle. Equally, in the inner circle make sure you do not plant a low growing plant next to a tall spreading herb because you will never find it.

This whole design can be incorporated in a small garden or on the edge of a vegetable garden to give colour throughout the growing season. As the majority of these herbs are annuals or die back into the ground, the autumn is an ideal time to give the garden a good feed by adding well rotted manure. This will encourage lots of leaves from the perennial herbs in the following season, and give a good kick start to the annuals when they are planted out in the following spring.

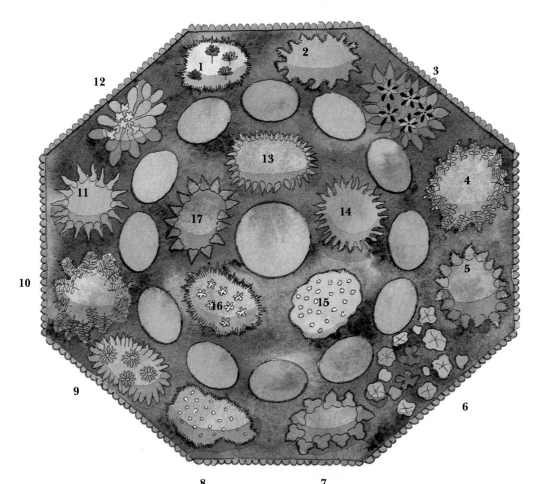

1	**Chives** *Allium schoenoprasum*	10	**Tarragon French** *Artemisia dracunculus*
2	**Caraway** *Carum carvi*	11	**Salad Rocket** *Eruca vesicaria*
3	**Borage** *Borago officinalis*	12	**Cowslips** *Primula veris*
4	**Salad Burnet** *Sanguisorba minor*	13	**Mint Spear** *Mentha spicata*
5	**Parsley French** *Petroselinum crispum hortense*	14	**Chicory** *Cichorium intybus*
6	**Nasturtium** *Tropaeolum majus*	15	**Thyme Lemon** *Thymus x citriodorus*
7	**Sorrel, Buckler Leaf** *Rumex scutatus*	16	**Chives, Garlic** *Allium tuberosum*
8	**Hyssop** *Hyssopus officinalis*	17	**Red Orach** *Atriplex hortensis* 'Rubra'
9	**Marigold Pot** *Calendula officinalis*		

COOK'S HERB GARDEN

The best site for a culinary herb bed is a sunny area accessible to the kitchen. The importance of this is never clearer than when it is raining. There is no way that you will go out and cut fresh herbs if they are a long way away and difficult to reach.

Another important factor is that the sunnier the growing position, the better the flavour of the herbs. This is because the sun brings the oils to the surface of the leaf of herbs such as sage, coriander, rosemary, basil, oregano and thyme.

The cook's herb garden could be grown in the ground or in containers. If in the ground, make sure that the site is very well drained. Position a paving stone near each herb so that it can be easily reached for cutting, weeding and feeding and also to help contain the would-be rampant ones, such as the mints.

Alternatively, the whole design could be adapted to be grown in containers. I have chosen only a few of the many varieties of culinary herb. If your favourite is missing, either add it to the design or substitute it for one of my choice.

1 **Mint Ginger** *Mentha x gracilis*
2 **Chervil** *Anthriscus cerefolium*
3 **Coriander** *Coriandrum sativum*
4 **Parsley French** *Petroselinum crispum hortense*
5 **Chives** *Allium schoenoprasum*
6 **Rosemary Corsican** *Rosmarinus officinalis* 'Corsican Blue'
7 **Thyme Garden** *Thymus vulgaris*
8 **Angelica** *Angelica archangelica*
9 **Fennel** *Foeniculum vulgare*
10 **Winter Savory** *Satureja montana*
11 **Basil Greek** *Ocimum basilicum minimum var.* 'Greek'
12 **Sorrel Buckler Leaf** *Rumex scutatus*
13 **Bay** *Laurus nobilis*
14 **Sweet Cicely** *Myrrhis odorata*
15 **Garlic** *Allium sativum*
16 **Oregano Greek** *Origanum vulgare spp*
17 **Tarragon French** *Artemisia dracunculus*
18 **Lovage** *Levisticum officinale*
19 **Chives, Garlic** *Allium tuberosum*
20 **Lemon Balm** *Melissa officinalis*
21 **Mint Moroccan** *Mentha spicata* 'Moroccan'
22 **Dill** *Anethum graveolens*
23 **Parsley** *Petroselinum crispum*
24 **Thyme Lemon** *Thymus x citriodorus*
25 **Marjoram Sweet** *Origanum majorana*

Allium schoenoprasum

CHIVES

From the family Liliaceae

Chives is the only member of the onion group found wild in Europe, Australia and North America, where it thrives in temperate and warm to hot regions. Although one of the most ancient of all herbs, chives were not cultivated in European gardens until the 16th century.

Chives were a favourite in China as long ago as 3,000 BC. They were enjoyed for their delicious mild onion flavour and used as an antidote to poison and to stop bleeding. Their culinary virtues were first reported to the West by the explorer and traveller, Marco Polo. During the Middle Ages they were sometimes known as rush-leeks, from the Greek 'schoinos' meaning rush and 'parson' meaning 'leek'.

Chives
Allium schoenoprasum

Chives *Allium schoenoprasum*

SPECIES

Allium schoenoprasum
Chives
Hardy perennial. Ht 30cm (12in). Purple globular flowers all summer. Leaves green and cylindrical. Apart from being a good culinary herb it makes an excellent edging plant.

Allium schoenoprasum 'fine leafed form'
Extra Fine Leafed Chives
Hardy perennial. Ht 20cm (8in), Purple globular flowers all summer. Very narrow cylindrical leaves, not as coarse as standard chives. Good for culinary usage.

Allium schoenoprasum 'white form'
White Chives
Hardy perennial. Ht 20cm (8in). White globular flowers all summer. Cylindrical green leaves. A cultivar of ordinary chives and very effective in a silver garden. Good flavour.

Allium schoenoprasum roseum
Pink Chives
Hardy perennial. Ht 20cm (8in). Pink flowers all summer. Cylindrical green leaves. Also a cultivar of ordinary chives, its pink flowers can look a bit insipid if planted too close to the purple flowered variety. Good in flower arrangements.

Garlic Chive flower
Allium tuberosum

Allium tuberosum
Garlic Chives (Chinese chives)
Hardy perennial. Ht 40cm (16in). White flowers all summer. Leaf mid-green, flat and solid with a sweet garlic flavour when young. As they get older the leaf becomes tougher and the taste coarser.

CULTIVATION

Propagation
Seed
Easy from seed, but they need a temperature of 19°C (65°F) to germinate, so if sowing outside, wait until late spring for the soil to be warm enough. I recommend starting this plant in plug trays with bottom heat in early spring. Sow about 10-15 seeds per 3cm (1in) cell. Transplant either into pots or into the garden when the soil has warmed.

Division
Every few years in the spring lift clumps (made up of small bulbs) and replant in 6-10 bulb-clumps, 15cm (6ins) apart, adding fresh compost or manure.

Pests and Diseases
Greenfly may be a problem on pot-grown herbs. Wash off gently under the tap or use a liquid horticultural soap. Be diligent, for aphids can hide deep down among the bulbs.

Cool wet autumns may produce downy mildew; the leaves will become velvety and die back from the tips. Dig up, split and re-pot affected plants, at the same time cutting back all the growth to prevent the disease spreading.

Chives can also suffer from rust. As this is a virus it is essential to cut back diseased growth immediately and burn it. DO NOT COMPOST. If very bad, remove the plant and burn it all. Do not plant any rust prone plants in that area.

Maintenance
Spring: Clear soil around emerging established plants. Feed with liquid fertilizer. Sow seeds
Summer: Remove the flower stem before flowering to increase leaf production.
Autumn: Prepare soil for next year's crop. Dig up a small clump, pot, bring inside for forcing.
Winter: Cut forced chives and feed regularly.

Garden Cultivation
Chives are fairly tolerant regarding soil and position, but produce the best growth planted 15cm (6in) from other plants in a rich moist soil and in a fairly sunny position. If the soil is poor they will turn yellow and then brown at the tips. For an attractive edging, plant at a distance of 10cm (4in) and allow to flower. Keep newly transplanted plants well watered in the spring, and in the summer make sure that they do not dry out, otherwise the leaves will quickly shrivel. Chives die right back into the ground in winter, but a winter cutting can be forced by digging up a clump in autumn, potting it into a rich mix of compost (bark, peat mix), and placing it somewhere warm with good light.

Harvest
Chives may be cut to within 3cm (1in) of the ground 4 times a year to maintain a supply of succulent fresh leaves. Chives do not dry well. Refrigerated leaves in a sealed plastic bag will retain crispness for seven days. Freeze chopped leaves in ice cubes for convenience.
  Cut flowers when they are fully open before the colour fades for use in salads and sauces.

MEDICINAL

The leaves are mildly antiseptic and when sprinkled onto food they stimulate the appetite and promote digestion.

CONTAINER GROWING

Chives grow well in pots or on a window sill and flourish in a window box if partially shaded. They need an enormous quantity of water and occasional liquid feed to stay green and succulent. Remember too that, being bulbs, chives need some top growth for strengthening and regeneration, so do not cut away all the leaves if you wish to use them next season. Allow to die back in winter if you want to use it the following spring. A good patio plant, easy to grow, but not particularly fragrant.

COMPANION PLANTING

Chives planted next to apple trees prevent scab, and when planted next to roses can prevent black spot. Hence the saying, 'Chives next to roses creates poses'.

OTHER USES

Chives are said to prevent scab infection on animals.

CULINARY

Add chives at the end of cooking or the flavour will disappear. They are delicious freshly picked and snipped as a garnish or flavour in omelettes or scrambled eggs, salads and soups. They can be mashed into soft cheeses or sprinkled onto grilled meats. Add to sour cream as a filling for jacket potatoes.

Chive Butter
Use in scrambled eggs, omelettes and cooked vegetables and with grilled lamb or fish or on jacket potatoes.

100g/4oz/½cup butter
4 tablespoons chopped chives
1 tablespoon lemon juice
Salt and pepper

Cream the chives and softened butter together until well mixed. Beat in the lemon juice and season to taste. Cover and cool the butter in the refrigerator until ready to use; it will keep for several days.

Anethum graveolens

DILL

Also known as Dillweed and Dillseed. From the family Umbelliferae.

A native of southern Europe and western Asia, dill grows wild in the cornfields of Mediterranean countries and also in North and South America. The generic name 'Anethum' derives from the Greek 'Anethon'. 'Dill' is said to come from the Anglo-Saxon 'dylle' or the Norse 'dilla', meaning to soothe or lull. Dill was found amongst the names of herbs used by Egyptian doctors 5,000 years ago and the remains of the plant have been found in the ruins of Roman buildings in Britain.

It is mentioned in the Gospel of St Matthew, where it is suggested that herbs were of sufficient value to be used as a tax payment – oh that that were true today! 'Woe unto you, Scribes and Pharisees, hypocrites! for ye pay tithe of mint and dill and cumin, and have omitted the weightier matters of the law.'

During the Middle Ages dill was prized as protection against witchcraft. While magicians used it in their spells, lesser mortals infused it in wine to enhance passion. It was once an important medicinal herb for treating coughs and headaches, as an ingredient of ointments and for calming infants with whooping cough – dill water or gripe water is still called upon today. Early settlers took dill to North America, where it came to be known as the 'Meeting House Seed', because the children were given it to chew during long sermons to prevent them feeling hungry.

SPECIES

Anethum graveolens
Dill
Annual. Ht 60-150cm (2-5ft), spread 30cm (12in). Tiny yellow/green flowers in flattened umbel clusters in summer. Fine aromatic feathery green leaves.

CULTIVATION

Propagation
Seed
Seed can be started in early spring under cover, using pots or plug trays. Do not use seed trays, as it does not like being transplanted, and if it gets upset it will bolt and miss out the leaf-producing stage.

The seeds are easy to handle, being a good size. Place 4 per plug or evenly spaced on the surface of a pot, and cover with Perlite. Germination takes 2-4 weeks, depending on the warmth of the surrounding area. As soon as the seedlings are large enough to handle, the air and soil temperatures have started to rise and there is no threat of frost, plant out 28cm (9in) apart.

Garden Cultivation
Keep dill plants well away from fennel, otherwise they will cross pollinate and their individual flavours will become muddled. Dill prefers a well-drained, poor soil in full sun. Sow mid-spring into shallow drills on a prepared site, where they will be harvested. Protect from wind. When the plants are

Dill *Anethum graveolens*

large enough to handle, thin out to a distance of 20cm (8in) to give plenty of room for growth. Make several small sowings in succession so that you have a supply of fresh leaves throughout the summer. The seed is viable for 3 years.

The plants are rather fragile and it may be necessary to provide support. Twigs pushed into the ground around the plant and enclosed with string or raffia will give better results than attempting to stake each plant individually.

In very hot summers, make sure that the plants are watered regularly or they will run to seed. There is no need to liquid feed, as this only promotes soft growth and in turn encourages pests and disease.

Pests and Diseases
Watch out for greenfly in crowded conditions. Treat with a liquid horticultural soap if necessary. Be warned, slugs love dill plants.

Maintenance
Spring: Sow the seeds successively for a leaf crop.
Summer: Feed plants with a liquid fertilizer after cutting to promote new growth.
Autumn (early): Harvest seeds.
Winter: Dig up all remaining plants. Make sure all the seed heads have been removed before you compost the stalks, as the seed is viable for 3 years. If you leave the plants to self-seed they certainly will, and they will live up to their other name of Dillweed.

Harvest

Pick leaves fresh for eating at any time after the plant has reached maturity. Since it is quick-growing, this can be within 8 weeks of the first sowing.

Although leaves can be dried, great care is needed and it is better to concentrate on drying the seed for storage.

Cut the stalks off the flower heads when the seed is beginning to ripen. Put the seed heads upside down in a paper bag and tie the top of the bag. Put in a warm place for a week. The seeds should then separate easily from the husk when rubbed in the palm of the hand. Store in an airtight container and the seeds will keep their flavour very well.

CONTAINER GROWING

Dill can be grown in containers, in a sheltered corner with plenty of sun. However, it will need staking. The art of growing it successfully is to keep cutting the plant for use in the kitchen. That way you will promote new growth and keep the plant reasonably compact. The drawback is that it will be fairly short-lived, so you will have to do successive sowings in different pots to maintain a supply. I do not recommend growing dill indoors – it will get leggy, soft and prone to disease.

MEDICINAL

Dill is an antispasmodic and calmative. Dill tea or water is a popular remedy for an upset stomach, hiccups or insomnia, for nursing

mothers to promote the flow of milk, and as an appetite stimulant. It is a constituent of gripe water and other children's medicines because of its ability to ease flatulence and colic.

CULINARY

Dill is a culinary herb that improves the appetite and digestion. The difference between dill leaf and dill seed lies in the degree of pungency. There are occasions when the seed is better because of its sharper flavour. It is used as a flavouring for soup, lamb stews and grilled or boiled fish. It can also add spiciness to rice dishes, and be combined with white wine vinegar to make dill vinegar.

Dill leaf can be used generously in many dishes, as it enhances rather than dominates the flavour of food.

Before it sets seed, add one flowering head to a jar of pickled gherkins, cucumbers and cauliflowers for a flavour stronger than dill leaves but fresher than seeds. In America these are known as dill pickles.

Gravlax – the traditional Scandinavian dish of salmon and dill

Gravlax
Salmon marinaded with dill

This is a traditional Scandinavian dish of great simplicity and great merit. Salmon treated in this way will keep for up to a week in the refrigerator.

420-800g (1½-2lb) salmon, middle cut or tail piece
1 heaped tablespoon sea salt
1 rounded tablespoon caster sugar
1 teaspoon crushed black peppercorns
1 tablespoon brandy (optional)
1 heaped tablespoon fresh dill

Have the salmon cleaned, scaled, bisected lengthways and filleted. Mix remaining ingredients together and put some of the mixture into a flat dish (glass or enamel) large enough to take the salmon. Place one piece of salmon skin side down on the bottom of the dish, spread more of the mixture over the cut side. Add the second piece of salmon, skin up, and pour over the remaining mixture. Cover with foil and place a plate or wooden board larger than the area of the salmon on top. Weigh this down with

weights or heavy cans. Put in the refrigerator for 36-72 hours. Turn the fish completely every 12 hours or so and baste (inside surfaces too) with the juices.

To serve, scrape off all the mixture, pat the fish dry and slice thinly and at an angle. Serve with buttered rye bread and a mustard sauce called Gravlaxsas:

4 tablespoons mild, ready-made Dijon mustard
1 teaspoon mustard powder
1 tablespoon caster sugar
2 tablespoons white wine vinegar

Mix all the above together, then slowly add 6 tablespoons of vegetable oil until you have a sauce the consistency of mayonnaise. Finally stir in 3 to 4 tablespoons of chopped dill.

Alternatively, substitute a mustard and dill mayonnaise.

OTHER USES

Where a salt-free diet must be follwed, the seed, whole or ground, is a valuable replacement. Try chewing the seeds to clear up halitosis and sweeten the breath. Crush and infuse seeds to make a nail-strengthening bath.

Dill vinegar

Anthriscus cerefolium

CHERVIL

From the family Umbelliferae

Native to the Middle East, South Russia and the Caucasus and cultivated in warm temperate climates, it is now occasionally found growing wild.

Almost certainly brought to Britain by the Romans, it is one of the Lenten herbs thought to have blood-cleansing and restorative properties. It was eaten in quantity in those days, especially on Maundy Thursday.

Gerard, the Elizabethan physician who superintended Lord Burleigh's gardens, wrote in his Herbal of 1636, 'The leaves of sweet chervil are exceeding good, wholesome and pleasant among other salad herbs, giving the taste of Anise seed unto the rest.'

Chervil *Anthriscus cerefolium*

SPECIES

Anthriscus cerefolium
Chervil
Hardy annual (some consider it to be a biennial). Ht 30-60cm (1-2ft), spread 30cm (12in). Flowers, tiny and white, grow in clusters from spring to summer. Leaves, light green and fern-like, in late summer may take on a purple tinge. When young it can easily be confused with cow parsley. However, cow parsley is a perennial and eventually grows much taller and stouter, its large leaves lacking the sweet distinctive aroma of chervil.

Anthriscus cerefolium crispum
Chervil curly leafed
Hardy annual. Grows like the ordinary chervil except that, in my opinion, the leaf has an inferior flavour.

CULTIVATION

Propagation
Seed
The medium-size seed germinates rapidly as the air and soil temperatures rise in the spring provided the seed is fresh (it loses viability after about a year). Young plants are ready for cutting 6-8 weeks after sowing, thereafter continuously providing leaves as long as the flowering stems are removed.

Seed in prepared plug trays if you prefer, and cover with Perlite. Pot on to containers with a minimum 12cm (5in) diameter. But as a typical *Umbelliferae*, with a long tap root, chervil does not like being transplanted, so keep this to a minimum. It can in fact be sown direct into a 12cm (5in) pot, growing it, like mustard and cress, as a cut-and-come-again crop.

Pests and Diseases

Chervil can suffer from greenfly. Wash off gently with a liquid horticultural soap. Do not blast off with a high pressure hose, as this will damage its soft leaves.

Maintenance

Spring: Sow seeds.
Summer: A late sowing in this season will provide leaves through winter, as it is very hardy. Protect from midday sun.
Autumn: Cloche autumn-sown plants for winter use.
Winter: Although chervil is hardy, some cloche protection is needed to ensure leaves in winter.

Garden Cultivation

The soil required is light with a degree of moisture retention. Plant spacing 23-30cm (9-12in). Semi-shade is best, because the problem with chervil is that it will burst into flower too quickly should the weather become sunny and hot and be of no use as a culinary herb. For this reason some gardeners sow between rows of other garden herbs or vegetables or under deciduous plants to ensure some shade during the summer months.

Harvest

Harvest leaves for use fresh when the plant is 6-8 weeks old or when 10cm (4in) tall, and all the year round if you cover with a cloche in winter. Otherwise, freezing is the best method of preservation, as the dried leaves do not retain their flavour.

CONTAINER GROWING

When grown inside in the kitchen chervil loses colour, gets leggy and goes floppy, so unless you are treating it as a cut-and-come-again plant, plant outside in a large container that retains moisture and is positioned in semi-shade.

Chervil looks good in a window box, but be sure that it gets shade at midday.

MEDICINAL

Leaves eaten raw are rich in Vitamin C, carotene, iron and magnesium. They may be infused to make a tea to stimulate digestion and alleviate circulation disorders, liver complaints and chronic catarrh, and fresh leaves may be applied to aching joints in a warm poultice.

CULINARY

It is one of the traditional 'fines herbes', indispensable to French cuisine and a fresh green asset in any meal, but many people in Britain are only now discovering its special delicate parsley-like flavour with a hint of Aniseed. This is a herb especially for winter use because it is easy to obtain fresh leaves and, as every cook knows, French or otherwise, 'Fresh is best'.

Use its leaf generously in salads, soups, sauces, vegetables, chicken, white fish and egg dishes. Add freshly chopped towards the end of cooking to avoid flavour loss.

In small quantities it enhances the flavour of other herbs. Great with vegetables.

OTHER USES

An infusion of the leaf can be used to cleanse skin, maintain suppleness and discourage wrinkles.

Chervil with broad beans

Artemisia dracunculus

TARRAGON

Also known as Estragon. From the family Compositae.

A native of southern Europe, tarragon is now found in dry areas of North America, Southern Asia and Siberia.

Dracunculus' means little dragon. Its naming could have occurred (via the Doctrine of Signatures) as a result of the shape of its roots, or because of its fiery flavour. Whatever, it was certainly believed to have considerable power to heal bites from snakes, serpents and other venomous creatures.

In ancient times the mixed juices of tarragon and fennel made a favourite drink for the Kings of India.

In the reign of Henry VIII, tarragon made its way into English gardens, and the rhyme, 'There is certain people, and certain herbs, that good digestion disturbs,' could well be associated with tarragon. I love, too, the story that Henry VIII divorced Catherine of Aragon for her reckless use of tarragon.

SPECIES

Artemisia dracunculus
French Tarragon
Half-hardy perennial. Ht 90cm (3ft), spread 45cm (18in). Tiny, insignificant, yellow flowerheads are borne in sprays in summer but rarely produce ripe seed sets except in warm climates. The leaves are smooth dark green, long and narrow, and have a very strong flavour.

Artemisia dracunculoides
Russian Tarragon
Hardy perennial. Ht 1.2m (4ft), spread 45cm (18in). Tiny, insignificant, yellow flowerheads are borne in sprays in summer. The leaves are slightly coarser and green in colour, their shape long and narrow. This plant originates from Siberia, which also explains why it is so hardy.

CULTIVATION

Propagation
Seed
Only the Russian variety produces viable seed. A lot of growers are propagating and selling it to the unsuspecting public as French tarragon. If you really want Russian tarragon, sow the small seed in spring, into prepared seed or plug trays, using the bark, peat, grit compost. No extra heat required. When the young plants are large enough to handle, transfer to the garden, 60cm (24in) apart.

Cuttings
Both French and Russian tarragon can be propagated by cuttings.
Roots: Dig up the underground runners in spring when the frosts are finished, pull them apart; do

not cut. You will notice growing nodules, these will reproduce in the coming season. Place a small amount of root – 8-10cm (3-4in) – each with a growing nodule, in a 8cm (3in) pot, and cover with compost. Use the bark, grit, peat mix and place in a warm, well ventilated place. Keep watering to a minimum. When well rooted, plant out in the garden after hardening off, 60cm (24in) apart.

It is possible to take softwood cuttings of the growing tips in summer. You will need to keep the leaves moist, but the compost on the dry side. It works best under a misting unit with a little bottom heat 15°C (60°F).

Division
Divide established plants of either variety in the spring.

Pests and Diseases
Recently there has been a spate of rust developing on French tarragon. When buying a plant, look for tell tale signs – small rust spots on the underneath of a leaf. If you have a plant with rust, dig it up, cut off all foliage carefully, and bin the leaves. Wash the roots free from soil, and pot up into fresh sterile soil. If this fails, place the dormant roots in hot water after washing off all the compost. The temperature of the water should be 40-46°C (105-115°F); over 46°C will damage the root. Leave the roots in the hot water for 5 minutes then replant in a new place in the garden.

Maintenance
Spring: Sow Russian tarragon seeds if you must. Divide established plants. Take root cuttings.
Summer: Remove flowers.
Autumn: Pot up pieces of French tarragon root as insurance.
Winter: Protect French tarragon. As the plant dies back into the ground in winter it is an ideal candidate for either agricultural fleece, straw or a deep mulch.

Garden Cultivation
French Tarragon has the superior flavour of the two and is the most tender. It grows best in a warm dry position, and will need protection in winter. It also dislikes humid conditions. The plant should be renewed every 3 years because the flavour deteriorates as the plant matures.

Russian tarragon is fully hardy and will grow in any conditions. There is a myth going around that it improves the longer it is grown in 1 place. This is untrue, it gets coarse. It is an extremely tolerant of most soil types, but prefers a sunny position, 60cm (2ft) away from other plants.

Harvest
Pick sprigs of French tarragon early in the season to make vinegar.

Pick leaves for fresh use throughout the growing season. For freezing it is best to pick the leaves in the mid-summer months.

Container Growing

French tarragon grows well in containers. Use the bark, grit mix of compost. As it produces root runners, choose a container to give it room to grow so that it will not become pot bound. At all times make sure the plant is watered, and in the daytime, not at night. It hates having wet roots. Keep feeding to a minimum; overfeeding produces fleshy leaves with a poor flavour; be mean. In winter, when the plant is dormant, do not water, keep the compost dry and the container in a cool, frost-free environment.

Culinary

Without doubt this is among the Rolls Royces of the culinary herb collection. Its flavour promotes appetite and complements so many dishes – chicken, veal, fish, stuffed tomatoes, rice dishes, and salad dressings, and of course is the main ingredient of Sauce Bernaise.

Chicken Salad with tarragon and grapes
Serves 4-6

1 1.3 kg (3lb) cooked chicken
150ml (5fl oz) mayonnaise
75ml (3fl oz) double cream
1 heaped teaspoon fresh chopped tarragon (½ teaspoon dried)
3 spring onions, finely chopped
100g (4oz) green grapes (seedless if not de-piped)
1 small lettuce
A few sprigs water cress
Salt and pepper

Remove the skin from the chicken and all the chicken from the bones. Slice the meat into longish pieces and place in a bowl.

In another bowl mix the mayonnaise with the cream, the chopped tarragon, and the finely chopped spring onions. Pour this mixture over the chicken and mix carefully together. Arrange the lettuce on a dish and spoon on the chicken mixture. Arrange the grapes and the water cress around it.

Serve with jacket potatoes or rice salad.

Medicinal

No modern medicinal use. Formerly used for toothache. If nothing else is available, a tea made from the leaves is said to overcome insomnia.

Coriandrum sativum

CORIANDER

Also known as Chinese Parsley, Yuen Sai, Pak Chee, Fragrant Green, Dhania (seed), Dhania Pattar and Dhania Sabz (leaves). From the family Umbelliferae.

A native of southern Europe and the Middle East, coriander was a popular herb in England up until Tudor times. Early European settlers in America included seed among the beloved items they took to the New World, as did Spaniards into Mexico.

Coriander has been cultivated for over 3,000 years. Seeds have been found in tombs from the 21st Egyptian Dynasty (1085-945 BC). The herb is mentioned in the Old Testament – 'when the children of Israel were returning to their homeland from slavery in Egypt, they ate manna in the wilderness and the manna was as coriander seeds' – and it is still one of the traditional bitter herbs to be eaten at the Passover when the Jewish people remember that great journey.

Coriander was brought to Northern Europe by the Romans who, combining it with cumin and vinegar, rubbed it into meat as a preservative. The Chinese once believed it bestowed immortality and in the Middle Ages it was put in love potions as an aphrodisiac. Its name is said to be derived from 'koris', Greek for 'bedbug', since the plant smells strongly of the insect.

Coriander *Coriandrum sativum*

Coriander *Coriandrum sativum*

SPECIES

Coriandrum sativum
Coriander
Tender annual. Ht 60cm (24in). White flowers in the summer. The first and lower leaves are broad and scalloped, with a strong, strange scent. The upper leaves are finely cut and have a different and yet more pungent smell. The whole plant is edible. This variety is good for leaf production.

Coriandrum sativum 'Cilantro'
Tender annual. Ht 60cm (24in). Much as **C. sativum**; whitish flowers in summer; also suitable for leaf production.

Coriandrum sativum 'Morocco'
Tender annual. Ht 70cm (28ins). Flowers white with a slight pink tinge in summer. This variety is best for seed production.

CULTIVATION

Propagation
Coriander is grown from seed. Thinly sow its large seed directly into the soil in shallow drills. Lightly cover with fine soil or compost, and water in. Look for results after a period of between 5 and 10 days. Seed sowing may be carried out as often as required between early spring (under glass), and late autumn. When large enough to handle, thin out the seedlings to leave

Coriander seeds

room for growth.

Sowing into seed trays is not recommended because coriander plants do not transplant well once the tap root is established. If they get upset they bolt straight into flower, missing out the leaf production stage.

If a harvest of fresh leaves is required, space the plants 5cm (2in) apart; if of seed, 23cm (9in) apart.

Pests and Diseases

Being a highly aromatic plant coriander is usually free from pests. In exceptional circumstances it is attacked by green fly. If so, do not be tempted to pressure hose the pests off, which it will destroy the leaves. Either wash off gently under the tap, and shake the plant gently to remove excess water on the leaves, or use a liquid horticultural soap.

Maintenance

Spring: Sow seeds.
Summer: Sow seeds, cut leaves.
Autumn: Cut seed heads. Sow autumn crop in mild climates. Dig up old plants.
Winter: Once the seed heads have been collected, the plant should be pulled up.

Garden Cultivation

Coriander grows best in a light, well-drained soil, a sunny position and a dry atmosphere. In fact it is difficult to grow in damp or humid areas and needs a good dry summer at the very least if a reasonable crop is to be obtained.

Plant out in cool climates when there is no threat of frost, making sure the final position is nowhere near fennel, which seems to suffer in its presence.

When the plant reaches maturity and the seed set and begin to ripen, the plant tends to loll about on its weak stem and needs staking. On ripening, the seeds develop a delightful orangy scent, and are used widely as a spice and a condiment. For this reason alone, and because the flavour of home-grown seeds is markedly superior to those raised commercially, coriander deserves a place in the garden. If you live in a mild, frost free climate, sow in the autumn for an over-winter crop; but make sure the plants are in full sunlight.

Harvest

Pick young leaves any time. They should be 10cm (4in) in height and bright green.

Watch seed heads carefully, as they ripen suddenly and will fall without warning. Cut the flower stems as the seed smell starts to become pleasant. Cover bunches of about 6 heads together in a paper bag. Tie the top of the bag and hang it upside down in a dry, warm, airy place. Leave for roughly 10 days. The seeds should come away from the husk quite easily and be stored in an airtight container. Coriander seeds keep their flavour well.

CONTAINER GROWING

Coriander can be grown in containers inside with diligence or outside on the windowsill or patio, but for a confined space inside it is not the best choice. Until the seeds ripen the whole plant has an unpleasant smell. Also, being an annual it has a short season. The only successful way to maintain it in a pot is to keep picking the mature leaves. However, if you do decide to grow coriander in a container ensure good drainage with plenty of chippings or broken pot pieces; use a bark, peat compost; and do not over-water in the evening. Like many herbs, coriander does not like wet feet.

CULINARY

The leaves and ripe seeds have two distinct flavours. The seeds are warmly aromatic, the leaves have an earthy pungency.

Coriander seeds are used regularly in Garam Masala (a mixture of spices) and in curries. Use ground seed in tomato chutney, ratatouille, frankfurters, curries, also in apple pies, cakes, biscuits and marmalade. Add whole seeds to soups, sauces and vegetable dishes.

Add fresh lower leaves to curries, stews, salads, sauces and as a garnish. Delicious in salads, vegetables and poultry dishes. A bunch of coriander leaves with a vinaigrette dressing goes particularly well with hard boiled eggs.

Mushrooms and Coriander
Serves 2

500g (1lb) button mushrooms
2 tablespoons cooking oil
2 teaspoons coriander seeds
1 clove garlic
2 tablespoons tomato purée
300 ml (½ pint) dry white wine
salt and pepper
coriander leaf for garnish

Wipe mushrooms and slice in half. Put the oil, wine, coriander seeds and garlic in a large saucepan. Bring to the boil and cover and simmer for 5 minutes. Add the mushrooms and tomato purée. Cook for 5 minutes, by which time the vegetables should be tender. Remove the mushrooms and put in a serving dish. Boil the liquid again for 5 minutes and reduce it by half. Pour over the mushrooms. When cool, sprinkle with some chopped coriander leaf.

Levisticum officinale

LOVAGE

Also known as Love Parsley, Sea Parsley, Lavose, Liveche. Smallage and European Lovage. From the family Umbelliferae.

This native of the Mediterranean can now be found naturalized throughout the temperate regions of the world, including Australia, North America and Scandinavia.

Lovage was used by the ancient Greeks, who chewed the seed to aid digestion and relieve flatulence. Knowledge of it was handed down to Benedictine monks by the Romans, who prescribed the seeds for the same complaints. In Europe a decoction of lovage was reputedly a good aphrodisiac that no witch worthy of the name could be without. The name is likely to have come from the Latin 'ligusticum', after Liguria in Italy, where the herb grew profusely.

Because lovage leaves have a deodorising and antiseptic effect on the skin, they were laid in the shoes of travellers in the Middle Ages to revive their weary feet, like latter-day odour eaters.

Lovage *Levisticum officinale*

SPECIES

Levisticum officinale
Lovage
Hardy perennial. Ht up to 2m (6ft), spread 1m (3ft) or more. Tiny, pale, greenish-yellow flowers in summer clusters. Leaves darkish green, deeply divided, and large toothed.
A close relation, **Ligusticum scoticum**, shorter with white clusters of flowers, is sometimes called lovage. It can be used in the same culinary way, but lacks its strong flavour and the growth.

CULTIVATION

Propagation
Seed
Sow under protection in spring into prepared plug or seed trays and cover with Perlite; a bottom heat of 15°C (60°F) is helpful. When the seedlings are large enough to handle and after a period of hardening off, transplant into a prepared site in the garden 60cm (2ft) apart.

Division
The roots of an established plant can be divided in the spring or autumn. Make sure that each division has some new buds showing.

Pests and Diseases
Leaf miners are sometimes a problem. Watch out for the first tunnels, pick off the affected leaves and destroy them, otherwise broad dry patches will develop and the leaves will start to wither away. To control this, cut the plant right down to the ground, burning the affected shoots. Give the plant a feed and it will shoot with new growth. The young growth is just what one needs for cooking.

Maintenance
Spring: Divide established plants.
Summer: Clip established plants to encourage new shoots.
Autumn: Sow seed in garden.
Winter: No need for protection.

Garden Cultivation
Lovage prefers a rich, moist but well-drained soil. Prior to first planting, dig the ground over deeply and manure well. The site can be either in full sun or partial shade. Seeds are best sown in the garden in the autumn. When the seedlings are large enough, thin to

60cm (2ft) apart. It is important that lovage has a period of dormancy so that it can complete the growth cycle.

Lovage is a tall plant, so position it carefully. It will reach its full size in 3-5 years. To keep the leaves young and producing new shoots, cut around the edges of the clumps.

Harvest

After the plant has flowered the leaves tend to have more of a bitter taste so harvest in early summer. I personally believe that lovage does not dry that well and it is best to freeze it. (See page 241 and use the Parsley technique).

Harvest seed heads when the seeds start to turn brown. Pick them on a dry day, tie a paper bag over their heads, and hang upside down in a dry, airy place. Use, like celery seed, for winter soups.

Dig the root for drying in the autumn of the second or third season.

CONTAINER GROWING

Lovage is fine grown outside in a large container. To keep it looking good, keep it well-clipped. I do not advise letting it run to flower unless you can support it. Remember at flowering stage, even in a pot, it can be in excess of 1.5m (5ft) tall.

WARNING

As lovage is very good at reducing water retention, people who are pregnant or who have kidney problems should not take this herb medicinally.

Lovage soup

CULINARY

Lovage is an essential member of any culinary herb collection. The flavour is reminiscent of celery. It adds a meaty flavour to foods and is used in soups, stews and stocks. Also add fresh young leaves to salads, and rub on chicken, and round salad bowls.

Crush seeds in bread and pastries, sprinkle on salads, rice and mashed potato. If using the rootstock as a vegetable in casseroles, remove the bitter tasting skin.

Lovage Soup

Serves 4
25g (1oz) butter
2 medium onions, finely chopped
500g (1lb) potatoes, peeled and diced
4 tablespoons finely chopped lovage leaves
850ml (1¼ pints) chicken or vegetable stock
300ml (½ pint) milk or 1 cup cream
Grated nutmeg
Salt and pepper

Melt the butter in a heavy pan and gently sauté the onions and diced potatoes for 5 minutes until soft. Add the chopped lovage leaves and cook for 1 minute. Pour in the stock, bring to the boil, season with salt and pepper, cover and simmer gently until the potatoes are soft (about 15 minutes). Purée the soup through a sieve or liquidizer and return to a clean pan. Blend in the milk or cream, sprinkle on a pinch of nutmeg and heat through. Do not boil OR IT WILL CURDLE. Adjust seasoning. Delicious hot or cold. Serve garnished with chopped lovage leaves.

Lovage and Carrot

Serves 2

2 teaspoons chopped lovage leaves
3 carrots, grated
1 apple, grated
125g (5oz) plain yoghurt
2 tablespoons mayonnaise
1 teaspoon salt (if needed)
Lettuce leaves
1 onion sliced into rings
Chives

Toss together the grated carrots, apple, lovage, mayonnaise and yoghurt. Arrange the lettuce leaves on a serving dish and fill with the lovage mixture. Decorate with a few raw onions rings, chives and tiny lovage leaves.

Lovage as a Vegetable

Treat lovage as you would spinach. Use the young growth of the plant stalks and leaves. Strip the leaves from the stalks, wash, and cut the stalks up into segments. Bring a pan of water to the boil add the lovage, bring the water back to the boil, cover, and simmer for about 5-7 minutes until tender. Strain the water. Make a white sauce using butter, flour, milk, salt, pepper and grated nutmeg. Add the lovage. Serve and wait for the comments!

MEDICINAL

Lovage is a remedy for digestive difficulties, gastric catarrh and flatulence. I know of 1 recipe from the West Country – a teaspoon of lovage seed steeped in a glass of brandy, strained and sweetened with sugar. It is taken to settle an upset stomach!

Infuse either seed, leaf or root and take to reduce water retention. Lovage assists in the removal of waste products, acts as a deodorizer, and aids rheumatism.

Its deodorizing and antiseptic properties enable certain skin problems to respond to a decoction added to bath water. This is made with 45-60g (1½-2oz) of root stock in 600ml (1 pint) water. Add to your bath.

Lovage, brandy and sugar settles an upset stomach

Ocimum basilicum

BASIL

Also known as Common Basil, St Joseph Wort, and Sweet Basil. From the family Labiatae

Basil is native to India, the Middle East and some Pacific Islands. It has been cultivated in the Mediterranean for thousands of years, but the herb only came to Western Europe in the 16th century with the spice traders and to America and Australia with the early European settlers.

This plant is steeped in history and intriguing lore. Its common name is believed to be an abbreviation of Basilikon phuton, Greek for 'kingly herb', and it was said to have grown around Christ's tomb after the resurrection. Some Greek Orthodox churches use it to prepare their holy water, and put pots of basil below their altars. However, there is some question as to its sanctity – both Greeks and Romans believed that people should curse as they sow basil to ensure germination. There was even some doubt about whether it was poisonous or not, and in Western Europe it has been thought both to belong to the Devil and to be a remedy against witches. In Elizabethan times Sweet Basil was used as a snuff for colds and to clear the brain and deal with headaches, and in the 17th century Culpeper wrote of basil's uncompromising if unpredictable appeal – 'It either makes enemies or gains lovers but there is no in-between.'

SPECIES

Ocimum basilicum
Sweet Basil (Genovese)
Annual. Ht 45cm (18in). A strong scent. Green, medium-sized leaves. White flowers. Without doubt the most popular basil. Sweet basil comes from Genoa in the north of Italy, hence its local name, Genovese. Use sweet basil in pasta sauces and salads, especially with tomato. Combines very well with garlic. Do not let it flower if using for cooking.

Ocimum basilicum 'Cinnamon'
Cinnamon Basil
Annual. Ht 45cm (18in). Leaves olive/brown/green with a hint of purple, highly cinnamon-scented when rubbed. Flowers pale pink. Cinnamon basil comes from Mexico and is used in spicy dishes and salad dressings.

The distinctive leaves of Green Ruffles Basil

Ocimum basilicum var. citriodorum
Lemon Basil (Kemangie)
Annual. Ht 30cm (12in). Light, bright, yellowish green leaves, more pointed than other varieties, with a slight serrated edge. Flowers pale, whitish. Lemon basil comes from Indonesia, is tender in cooler climates, and susceptible to damping off. Difficult to maintain but well worth the effort. Both flowers and leaves have a lemon scent and flavour that enhance many dishes.

Cinnamon basil *Ocimum basilicum 'Cinnamon'*

Ocimum basilicum 'Green Ruffles'
Green Ruffles Basil
Annual. Ht 30cm (12in). Light green leaves, crinkly and larger than sweet basil. Spicy, aniseed flavour, good in salad dishes and combines well with stir-fry vegetables. But it is not, to my mind, an attractive variety. In fact the first time I grew it I thought its crinkly leaves had a bad attack of greenfly. Grow in pots and protect from any frost.

Ocimum basilicum var. minimum
Bush Basil
Annual. Ht 30cm (12in). Small green leaves, roughly half the size of sweet basil. Flowers small, scented and whitish. Spread from Chile throughout South America, where, in some countries, it is believed to belong to the pagan Goddess Erzulie and is carried both as a powerful protector against robbery and by young ladies to keep a lover's eye from roving. Excellent for growing in pots on the windowsill. Delicious added whole to green salads; goes well with ricotta cheese.

Ocimum basilicum var. minimum 'Greek'
Greek Basil (Fine-leaved Miniature)
Annual. Ht 23cm (9in). This basil has the smallest leaves, tiny replicas of the bush basil leaves but, despite their size, they have a good flavour. As its name depicts it originates from Greece. It is one of the easiest basils to look after and is especially good grown in a pot. Use leaves unchopped in all salads and in tomato sauces.

Ocimum basilicum neapolitanum
Lettuce-leaved Basil
Annual. Ht 45cm (18in). Leaves very large, crinkled, and with a distinctive flavour, especially good for pasta sauce. Originates in Naples region of Italy and needs a hot summer in cooler countries to be of any merit.

Ocimum basilicum 'Purple Ruffles'
Purple Ruffles Basil
Annual. Ht 30cm (12in). Very similar to straight purple basil (below), though the flavour is not as strong and the leaf is larger with a feathery edge. Flowers are pink. It can be grown in pots in a sunny position outside, but frankly it is a pain to grow because it damps off so easily.

Ocimum basilicum var. purpurascens
Purple Basil
Annual. Ht 30cm (12in) Strongly scented purple leaves. Pink flowers. Very attractive plant with a perfumed scent and flavour that is especially good with rice dishes. The dark purple variety that was developed in 1962 at the University of Connecticut represents something of a breakthrough in herb cultivation not least because, almost exclusively, herbs have escaped the attentions of the hybridizers. The variety was awarded the All American Medal by the seedsmen.

The many diverse shapes and colours of basil

Sacred basil *Ocimum tenuiflorum (sanctum)*

Ocimum 'Horapha'
Horapha Basil (Rau Que)
Annual. Ht 42cm (15in). Leaf olive/purplish. Stems red. Flowers with pink bracts. Aniseed in scent and flavour. A special culinary basil from Thailand. Use the leaves as a vegetable in curries and spicy dishes.

Ocimum tenuiflorum (sanctum)
Sacred Basil (Kha Prao Tulsi)
Annual. Ht 30cm (12in). A small basil with olive/purple leaves with serrated edges. Stems deep purple. Flowers mauve/pink. The whole plant has a marvellously rich scent. Originally from Thailand, where it is grown around Buddhist temples. Can be used in Thai cooking with stir-fry hot peppers, chicken, pork or beef. The Indian-related variety, *sanctum*, is considered kingly or holy by the Hindus, sacred to the Gods Krishna and Vishnu. Being held in reverence it was the chosen herb upon which to swear oaths in courts of Law. It was also used throughout the Indian subcontinent as a disinfectant where malaria was present.

CULTIVATION

Propagation
Seed

All basils can be grown from seed. Sow direct into pots or plug trays in early spring and germinate with warmth. Avoid using seed trays because basil has a long tap root and dislikes being transplanted. Plugs also help minimize damping off, to which all basil plants are prone (see below). Water well at midday in dry weather even when transplanted into pots or containers: basil hates going to bed wet. This minimizes the chances of damping off and will prevent root rot, a hazard when air temperature is still dropping at night.

Plant out seedlings when large enough to handle and the danger of frost has passed. The soil needs to be rich and well drained, and the situation warm and sheltered, preferably with sun at midday. However, prolific growth will only be obtained usually in the greenhouse or in large pots on a sunny patio. I suggest you plant basil in between tomato plants because:

1. being a good companion plant it repels flying insects
2. you will remember to use fresh basil with tomatoes
3. you will remember to water it
4. the situation will be warm and whenever you pick tomatoes you will tend to pick basil, which will encourage bushy growth and prevent it flowering, which in turn will stop the stems becoming woody and the flavour of its leaves bitter.

Pests and Diseases

Greenfly and whitefly may be a problem with pot grown plants. Wash off with liquid horticultural soap.

Seedlings are highly susceptible to damping off, a fungal disease encouraged by overcrowding in overly wet conditions in seed trays or pots. It can be prevented by sowing the seed thinly and widely and guarding against an over-humid atmosphere.

Maintenance

Spring: Sow seeds in early spring with warmth and watch out for damping off; plant out around the end of the season. Alternatively, sow directly into the ground after any frosts.
Summer: Keep pinching out young plants to promote new leaf growth and to prevent flowering. Harvest the leaves.
Autumn: Collect seeds of plants allowed to flower. Before first frosts, bring pots into the house and place on the windowsill. Dig up old plants and dig over the area ready for new plantings.

Garden Cultivation

Garden cultivation is only a problem in areas susceptible to frost and where it is not possible to provide for its great need for warmth and nourishment. In such areas plant out after the frosts have finished; choose a well drained, rich soil in a warm, sunny corner, protected from the wind.

Harvest

Pick leaves when young and always from the top to encourage new growth.

If freezing to store, paint both sides of each leaf with olive oil to stop it sticking to the next and to seal in its flavour.

If drying, do it as fast as you can. Basil leaves are some of the more difficult to dry successfully and I do not recommend it.

The most successful course, post-harvest, is to infuse the leaves in olive oil or vinegar. As well as being useful in your own kitchen, both the oil and the vinegar make great Christmas presents (see Preserving).

Gather flowering tops as they open in the summer and early autumn. Add fresh to salads, dry to potpourris.

CONTAINER GROWING

Basil is happy on a kitchen windowsill and in pots on the patio, and purple basil makes a good centrepiece in a hanging basket. In Europe basil is placed in pots outside houses to repel flies.

Water well at midday but do not over–water. If that is not possible water earlier in the day rather than later and again do not over-water.

OTHER USES

Keep it in a pot in the kitchen to act as a fly repellant, or crush a leaf and rub it on your skin, where the juice repels mosquitoes.

MEDICINAL

Once prescribed as a sedative against gastric spasms and as an expectorant and laxative, basil is rarely used in herbal medicines today. However, leaves added to food are an aid to digestion and if you put a few drops of basil's essential oil on a sleeve and inhale, it can allay mental fatigue. For those that need a zing it can also be used to make a very refreshing bath vinegar, which also acts as an antiseptic.

CULINARY

Basil has a unique flavour, so newcomers should use with discretion otherwise it will dominate other flavours. It is one of the few herbs to increase its flavour when cooked. For best results add at the very end of cooking.

Hints and ideas
1. Tear the leaves, rather than chop. Sprinkle over green salads or sliced tomatoes.
2. Basil combines very well with garlic. Tear into French salad dressing.
3. When cooking pasta or rice, heat some olive oil in a saucepan, remove from heat, add some torn purple basil, toss the pasta or rice in the basil and oil, and serve. Use lemon basil to accompany a fish dish – it has a sharp lemon/spicy flavour when cooked.
4. Add to a cold rice or pasta salad.
5. Mix low fat cream cheese with any of the basils and use in baked potatoes.
6. Basil does not combine well with strong meats such as goat or vension. However, aniseed basil is very good with stir fried pork.
7. Sprinkle on fried or grilled tomatoes while they are still hot as a garnish.
8. Very good with French bread and can be used instead of herb butter in the traditional hot herb loaf. The tiny leaves of Greek basil are best for this because you can keep them whole.
9. Sprinkle on top of pizzas.
10. Basil makes an interesting stuffing for chicken. Use sweet basil combined with crushed garlic, bread crumbs, lemon peel, beaten egg, and chopped nuts.

Pesto Sauce
One of the best known recipes for basil, here is a simple version for 4 people.

1 tablespoon pine nuts
4 tablespoons chopped basil leaves
2 cloves garlic
75g (3oz) Parmesan cheese
6 tablespoons sunflower oil or olive oil (not virgin)

Blend the pine nuts, basil and chopped garlic until smooth. Add the oil slowly and continue to blend the mixture until you have a thick paste. Season with salt to taste. Stir the sauce into the cooked and drained pasta and sprinkle with Parmesan cheese.

Pesto sauce will keep in a sealed container in the fridge for at least a week. It can also be frozen but it is important, as with all herbal mixtures, to wrap the container with at least two thickness of polythene to prevent the aroma escaping.

Pasta with Purple Ruffles Basil

Origanum

OREGANO &
MARJORAM

***Also known as Wild Marjoram, Mountain Mint, Winter Marjoram, Winter Sweet, Marjolaine and Origan.
From the family Labiatae.***

For the most part these are natives of the Mediterranean region. They have adapted to many countries, however, and a native form can now be found in many regions of the world, even if under different common names. For example, *Origanum vulgare* growing wild in Britain is called wild marjoram (the scent of the leaf is aromatic but not strong, the flowers are pale pink); while in Mediterranean countries wild *Origanum vulgare* is known as oregano (the leaf is green, slightly hairy and very aromatic, the flowers are similar to those found growing wild in Britain).

Oregano is derived from the Greek 'oros' meaning mountain and 'ganos' meaning joy and beauty. It therefore translates literally as 'joy of the mountain'. In Greece it is woven into the crown worn by bridal couples.

Pot Marjoram *Origanum onites*

According to Greek mythology, the King of Cyprus had a servant called Amarakos, who dropped a jar of perfume and fainted in terror. As his punishment the gods changed him into oregano, after which, if it was found growing on a burial tomb, all was believed well with the dead. Venus was the first to grow the herb in her garden.

Aristotle reported that tortoises, after swallowing a snake, would immediately eat oregano to prevent death, which gave rise to the belief that it was an antidote to poison.

The Greeks and Romans used it not only as scent after taking a bath and as a massage oil, but also as a disinfectant and preservative. More than likely they were responsible for the spread of this plant across Europe, where it became known as marjoram. The New Englanders took it to North America, where there arose a further confusion of nomenclature. Until the 1940s, common marjoram was called wild marjoram in America, but is now known as oregano. In certain parts of Mexico and the southern states of America, oregano is the colloquial name for a totally unrelated plant with a similar flavour.

Sweet marjoram, which originates from North Africa, was introduced into Europe in the 16th century and was incorporated in nosegays to ward off the plague and other pestilence.

Wild Marjoram
Origanum vulgare

SPECIES

Origanum amanum
Hardy perennial. Ht and spread 15-20cm (6-8in). Open, funnel-shaped, pale pink or white flowers borne above small heart-shaped, aromatic, pale green leaves. Makes a good alpine house plant. Dislikes a damp atmosphere.

Origanum x applei (heraceleoticum)
Winter Marjoram
Half-hardy perennial. Ht 23cm (9in), spread 30cm (12in). Small pink flowers. Very small aromatic leaves which, in the right conditions, are available all year round. Good to grow in a container.

Origanum dictamnus
Ditany of Crete
Hardy perennial. Ht 12-15cm (5-6in), spread 40cm (16in). Prostrate habit, purplish pink flowers that appear in hop-like clusters in summer. The leaves are white and woolly and grow on arching stems. Pretty little plant, quite unlike the other **origanums** in appearance. Tea made from the leaves is considered a panacea in Crete.

Golden Marjoram
Origanum vulgare 'Aureum'

Origanum 'Kent Beauty'
Hardy perennial. Ht 15-20cm (6-8in), spread 30cm (12in). Whorls of tubular pale pink flowers with darker bracts appear in summer on short spikes. Round, oval and aromatic leaves on trailing stems, which give the plant its prostrate habit and make it suitable for a wall or ledge. Decorative more than culinary.

Origanum laevigatum
Hardy perennial. Ht 23-30cm (9-12in), spread 20cm (8in). Summer profusion of tiny, tubular, cerise/pink/mauve flowers, surrounded by red/purple bracts. Aromatic, dark green leaves, which form a mat in winter. Decorative more than culinary.

Origanum laevigatum 'Herrenhausen'
Hardy perennial. Ht and spread 30cm (12in). Pink/mauve flowers which develop from deep purple buds in summer. Dark green, aromatic, slightly hairy leaves, with a pink tinge underneath. Decorative, and culinary when no other is available.

Greek Oregano
Origanum vulgare spp.

Origanum majorana (Origanum hortensis)
Sweet Marjoram
Also known as Knotted Marjoram or Knot Marjoram Half-hardy perennial. Grown as an annual in cool climates. Ht and spread 30cm (12in). Tiny white flowers in a knot. Round pale green leaves, highly aromatic. This is the best variety for flavour. Use in culinary recipes that state marjoram. The leaf is also good for drying, retaining a lot of its scent and flavour.

Origanum onites
Pot Marjoram
Hardy perennial. Ht and spread 45cm (18in). Pink/purple flowers in summer. Green aromatic leaves that form a mat in winter. Good grower with a nice flavour. Difficult to obtain the true seed; grows easily from cuttings, however.

Origanum rotundifolium
Hardy perennial. Ht 23-30cm (9-12in), spread 30cm (12in). Prostrate habit. The pale pink, pendant, funnel-shaped flowers appear in summer in whorls surrounded by yellow/green bracts. Leaves are small, round, mid-green, and aromatic. Decorative more than culinary.

Origanum vulgare
Oregano
Also known as Wild Marjoram
Hardy perennial. Ht and spread 45cm (18in). Clusters of tiny tubular mauve flowers in summer. Dark green, aromatic, slightly hairy leaves, which form a mat in winter. When grown in its native Mediterranean, it has a very pungent flavour, which bears little resemblance to that obtained in the cooler countries. When cultivated in the garden it becomes similar to pot marjoram.

Origanum vulgare spp.
Greek Oregano
Hardy perennial. Ht and spread 45cm (18in). Clusters of tiny tubular white flowers in summer. Grey/green hairy leaves, which are very aromatic and excellent to cook with.

Origanum vulgare 'Aureum'
Golden Marjoram
Hardy perennial. Ht and spread 45cm (18in). Clusters of tiny tubular mauve/pink flowers in summer. Golden, aromatic, slightly hairy leaves, which form a mat in winter. The leaves have a warm aromatic flavour when used in cooking; combines well with vegetables.

Compact Marjoram
Origanum vulgare 'Compactum'

Origanum vulgare 'Aureum Crispum'
Golden Curly Marjoram
Hardy perennial. Ht and spread 45cm (18in). Clusters of tiny tubular mauve/pink/white flowers in summer. Leaves, small, golden, crinkled, aromatic and slightly hairy, which form a mat in winter. The leaves have a slightly milder savoury flavour (sweeter and spicy) that combines well with vegetable dishes.

Origanum vulgare 'Compactum'
Compact Marjoram
Hardy perennial. Ht 15cm (6in), spread 30cm (12in). Lovely large pink flowers. Smallish green aromatic leaves, which form a mat in winter, have a deliciously warm flavour and combine well with lots of culinary dishes.

Origanum vulgare 'Gold Tip'
Gold Tipped Marjoram
Also known as Gold Splash Hardy perennial. Ht and spread 30cm (12in). Small pink flowers in summer. The aromatic leaves are green and yellow variegated. Choose the garden site carefully: shade prevents the variegation. The leaves have a mild savoury flavour.

Origanum vulgare 'Nanum'
Dwarf Marjoram
Hardy perennial. Ht 10cm (4in), spread 15cm (6in). White/pink flowers in summer. Tiny green aromatic leaves. It is a lovely, compact, neat little bush, great in containers and at the front of a herb garden. Good in culinary dishes.

CULTIVATION

Propagation
Seed
The following can be grown from seed: **Origanum vulgare**, **Origanum majorana**, **Origanum vulgare spp.** (Greek). The seed is very fine, so sow in spring into prepared seed or plug trays. Use the cardboard trick. Leave uncovered and give a bottom heat of 15°C (60°F). Germination can be erratic or 100 per cent successful. Watering is critical when the seedlings are young; keep the compost on the dry side. As the seed is so fine thin before pricking out to allow the plants to grow. When large enough, either pot on, using the bark, grit, peat mix of compost, or if the soil is warm enough and you have grown them in plugs, plant into the prepared garden.

Cuttings
Apart from the 3 species mentioned above, the remainder can only be propagated successfully by cuttings or division.
Softwood cuttings can be taken from the new growing tips of all the named varieties in spring. Use the bark, grit mix of compost.

Division
A number of varieties form a mat during the winter. These lend themselves to division. In spring, or after flowering, dig up a whole clump and pull sections gently away. Each will come away with its own root system. Replant as wanted.

Pests and Diseases
Apart from occasional frost damage, marjorams and oreganos, being aromatic, are mostly pest free.

Maintenance
Spring: Sow seeds. Divide established plants. Take softwood cuttings.
Summer: Trim after flowering to prevent plants becoming straggly. Divide established plants in late summer.
Autumn: Before they die down for winter, cut back the year's growth to within 6cm (2½in) of the soil.
Winter: Protect pot grown plants and tender varieties.

Garden Cultivation
Sweet marjoram and winter marjoram need a sunny garden site and a well-drained, dry, preferably chalk, soil. Otherwise plant them in containers. All the rest are hardy and adaptable, and will tolerate most soils as long as they are not waterlogged in winter. Plant gold varieties in some shade to prevent the leaves from scorching. For the majority, a good planting distance is 25cm (10in), closer if being used as an edging plant.

Harvest
Leaves
Pick leaves whenever available for use fresh. They can be dried or frozen, or be used to make oil or vinegar.

Flowers
The flowers can be dried just as they open for dried flower arrangements.

CONTAINER GROWING

The **Origanum** species look great in containers. Use the bark, grit, peat mix of compost. Make sure that they are not over-watered and that the gold and variegated forms get some shade at midday. Cut back after flowering and give them a liquid fertilizer feed.

CULINARY

Marjoram and oregano aid the digestion, and act as an antiseptic and as a preservative.
They are among the main ingredients of bouquet garni, and combine well with pizza, meat and tomato dishes, vegetables and milk-based desserts.

Red Mullet with Tomatoes and Oregano
Serves 4-6

4-6 red mullet, cleaned
3 tablespoons olive oil
1 medium onion, sliced
1 clove garlic, chopped
500g (1lb) tomatoes, peeled and chopped
1 green or red pepper, seeded and diced
1 teaspoon sugar
1 teaspoon chopped fresh oregano or ½ teaspoon dried oregano
Freshly milled salt and pepper
Oil for baking or shallow frying

Rinse the fish in cold water and drain on kitchen paper. Heat the olive oil in a pan and cook the onion and garlic slowly until golden brown; add the tomatoes, pepper, sugar and oregano, and a little salt and pepper.

Bring to the boil, then simmer for 20 minutes until thickened.
Bake or fry the fish. Brush them with oil, place in an oiled ovenproof dish and cook at a moderately hot temperature, 190°C (375°F, Gas Mark 5) for 7-8 minutes. Serve with the sauce.

MEDICINAL

This plant is one of the best antiseptics owing to its high Thymol content.
Marjoram tea helps ease bad colds, has a tranquil-lizing effect on nerves, and helps settle upset stomachs. It also helps to prevent sea sickness.
For temporary relief of toothache, chew the leaf or rub a drop of essential oil on the gums. A few drops of essential oil on the pillow will help you sleep.

OTHER USES

Make an infusion and add to the bath water to aid relaxation.

Red mullet with tomatoes and oregano

Eruca vesicaria

SALAD ROCKET

Also known as Rocquette. From the family Cruciferae.

This native of the Mediterranean has only recently found its way back into the British herb garden after an absence of a few hundred years. An annual salad plant with pungent tasting leaves, it is used a great deal in Southern France and Italy. It has been in continuous cultivation since the Romans, who prized the flavour of its leaves and seeds. In England the Elizabethans were extremely partial to it. Some fascinating past uses suggest that it should be taken before a whipping to alleviate the pain, and used as protection against bites of the shrew mouse and other venomous beasts.

SPECIES

Eruca vesicaria spp. Sativa
Salad Rocket
Half-hardy annual. Ht 60-90cm (2-3ft). The flowers are yellowish at first, then in the summer they become whiter with purple veins. The oval lanced-shaped leaves have a nutty flavour.

Salad Rocket *Eruca vesicaria*

CULTIVATION

Propagation
This herb is better grown direct in the garden.

Pests and Diseases
This herb rarely suffers from pests and diseases.

Maintenance
Spring: Sow seeds.
Summer: Pick like mad to prevent flowering.
Autumn: In mild climates sow seeds for winter salads.
Winter: In cooler climates use a cloche for protection.

Garden Cultivation
Sow seed in prepared rows in rich moist soil and a lightly shaded position. In warm countries, sow in autumn to ensure winter leaves. In cooler climates sow in early spring after the last frost, as in severe winters it may not survive. Thin the seedlings to 20cm (8in). It will be ready to pick within 6 to 8 weeks of sowing. It should be gathered before flowering. Be forewarned, late spring sowings are apt to run to seed quickly; if not picked sufficiently, the thin stems of cabbage flowers rise and flavour is lost from the leaves.

Harvest
Harvest leaf within 8 weeks of spring sowing, and keep cutting.

CONTAINER GROWING

Salad Rocket is not really suitable for growing in containers, but it is possible. Sow in spring directly into a pot or a window box. Use the bark, peat compost mix. Water and pick regularly. Do not use liquid fertilizer, as this makes the leaves too lush and bereft of flavour.

CULINARY

Add the leaves to all forms of salad. The younger leaves have a milder taste than the older ones, which have a definite peppery flavour. Leaves can also be added to sauces and to other vegetable dishes either raw or steamed. This herb is one of many leaves included in the Provençal salad mixture called mesclun.

Right: **Salad Rocket in flower**

Salad Rocket leaves in salad

MEDICINAL

At one time used medicinally in cough syrup.

Petroselinum

PARSLEY

Also known as Common Parsley, Garden Parsley and Rock Parsley. From the family Umbelliferae.

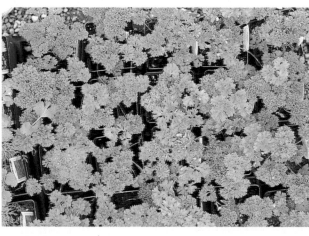

Parsley in pots

Best known of all garnishing herbs in the West. Native to central and southern Europe, in particular the Mediterranean region, now widely cultivated in several varieties throughout the world.

The Greeks had mixed feelings about this herb. It was associated with Archemorus, the Herald of Death, so they decorated their tombs with it. Hercules was said to have chosen parsley for his garlands, so they would weave it into crowns for victors at the Isthmian Games. But they did not eat it themselves, preferring to feed it to their horses. However, the Romans consumed parsley in quantity and made garlands for banquet guests to discourage intoxication and to counter strong odours.

It was believed that only a witch or a pregnant woman could grow it, and that a fine harvest was only ensured if the seeds were planted on Good Friday. It was also said that if parsley was transplanted, misfortune would descend upon the household.

Parsley *Petroselinum crispum*

SPECIES

Petroselinum crispum
Parsley
Hardy biennial. Ht 30-40cm (12-16in). Small creamy white flowers in flat umbels in summer. The leaf is brightish green and has curly toothed edges and a mild taste. It is mainly used as a garnish.

Petroselinum crispum hortense
French Parsley
Also known as Broad Leafed Parsley.
Hardy biennial. Ht 45-60cm (18-24in). Small creamy white flowers in flat umbels in summer. Flat dark green leaves with a stronger flavour than **P. crispum**. This is the one I recommend for culinary use.

Petroselinum crispum var. tuberosum
Hamburg Parsley
Also known as Turnip Rooted Parsley.
Perennial, grown as an annual. Root length up to 15cm (6in). Leaf, green and very similar to French parsley.
This variety, probably first developed in Holland, was introduced into England in the early 18th century, but it was only popular for 100 years. The plant is still frequently found in vegetable markets in France and Germany.
Warning: In the wild there is a plant called Fool's Parsley, **Aethusa cynapium**, which looks and smells to the novice like French parsley. Do not be tempted to eat it as it is extremely poisonous.

French Parsley
Petroselinum crispum hortense

CULTIVATION

Propagation
Seed
In cool climates, to ensure a succession of plants, sow seedlings under cover only in plug trays or pots. Avoid seed trays because, as with all *umbelliferae*, it hates being transferred. Cover with Perlite. If you have a heated propagator, a temperature of 18°C (65°F) will speed up germination. It takes 4-6 weeks without bottom heat and 2-3 weeks with. When the seedlings are large enough and the air and soil temperature have started to rise (about mid-spring), plant out 15cm (6in) apart in a prepared garden bed.

Pests and Diseases
Slugs love young parsley plants. There is a fungus which may attack the leaves. It produces first brown then white spots. Where this occurs the whole stock should be destroyed. Get some fresh seed.

Maintenance

Spring: Sow seed.
Summer: Sow seed. Cut flower heads as they appear on second-year plants.
Autumn: Protect plants for winter crop.
Winter: Protect plants for winter picking.

Garden Cultivation

Parsley is a hungry plant, it likes a good deep soil, not too light and not acid. Always feed the chosen site well in the previous autumn with well-rotted manure.

If you wish to harvest parsley all year round, prepare 2 different sites. For summer supplies, a western or eastern border is ideal because the plant needs moisture and prefers a little shade. For winter supplies, a more sheltered spot will be needed in a sunny position.

The seeds should be sown thinly, in drills 30-45cm (12-18in) apart and about 3cm (1in) deep. Germination is very slow. Keep the soil moist at all times, otherwise the seed will not germinate.

As soon as the seedlings are large enough, thin to 8cm (3in) and then 15cm (6in) apart. If at any time the leaves turn a bit yellow, cut back to encourage new growth and feed with a liquid fertilizer. At the first sign of flower heads appearing remove them if you wish to continue harvesting the leaves. Remember to water well during hot weather. In the second year parsley runs to seed very quickly. Dig it up as soon as the following year's crop is ready for picking, and remove it from the garden.

Hamburg or turnip parsley differs only in the respect that it is a root not a leaf crop. When the seedlings are large enough, thin to 20cm (8in) apart. Water well all summer. The root tends to grow more at this time of year, and unlike a lot of root crops the largest roots taste the best. Lift in late autumn, early winter. They are frost resistant.

Harvest

Pick leaves during first year for fresh use or for freezing (by far the best method of preserving parsley).

Dig up roots of Hamburg parley in the autumn of the first year and store in peat or sand.

CULINARY

Parsley is a widely used culinary herb, valued for its taste as well as its rich nutritional content. Cooking with parsley enhances the flavour of other foods and herbs. In bland food, the best flavour is obtained by adding it just before the end of cooking.

As so many recipes include parsley, here are some basic herb mixtures.

Fines Herbes

You will see this mentioned in a number of recipes and it is a classic for omelettes.

1 sprig parsley, chopped
1 sprig chervil, chopped
Some chives cut with scissors
1-2 leaves French tarragon

Chop up all the herbs finely and add to egg dishes.

Fish Bouquet Garni

2 sprigs parsley
1 spring French tarragon
1 sprig fennel (small)
2 leaves lemon balm

Tie the herbs together in a bundle and add to the cooking liquid.

Boil Hamburg parsley as a root vegetable or grate raw into salads. Use in soup mixes, the flavour resembles both celery and parsley.

CONTAINER GROWING

Parsley is an ideal herb for containers, it even likes living inside on the kitchen windowsill, as long as it is watered, fed, and cut. Use the bark, peat mix of compost. Curly parsley can look very ornamental as an edging to a large pot of nasturtiums. It can also be grown in hanging baskets, (keep well watered), window boxes (give it some shade in high summer), and containers. That brings me to the parsley pot, the one with six holes around the side. Do not use it. As I have already said, parsley likes moisture, and these containers dry out too fast, the holes in the side are small and make it very difficult to water, and the parsley has too big a tap root to be happy.

WARNING

Avoid medicinal use during pregnancy. There is an oil produced from parsley, but it should only be used under medical supervision.

MEDICINAL

All parsleys are a rich source of vitamins including Vitamin C. They are also high in iron and other minerals and contain the antiseptic chlorophyll.

It is a strong diuretic suitable for treating urinary infections as well as fluid retention. It also increases mothers' milk and tones the uterine muscle.

Parsley is a well known breath freshener, being the traditional antidote for the pungent smell of garlic. Chew raw, to promote a healthy skin.

Use in poultices as an antiseptic dressing for sprains, wounds and insect bites.

OTHER USES

A tea made from crushed seeds kills head lice vermin. Pour it over the head after washing and rinsing, wrap your head in a towel for 30 minutes and then allow to dry naturally. Equally, the seeds or leaves steeped in water can be used as a hair rinse.

Parsley tea

Rosmarinus

ROSEMARY

From the family Labiatae.

Rosemary is a shrub that originated in the Mediterranean area and is now widely cultivated throughout the temperate regions. The ancient Latin name means sea-dew. This may come from its habit of growing close to the sea and the dew-like appearance of its blossom at a distance. It is steeped in myth, magic and folk medicinal use. One of my favourite stories about Rosemary comes from Spain. It relates that originally the blue flowers were white. When the Holy family fled into Egypt, the Virgin Mary had to hide from some soldiers, so she spread her cloak over a rosemary bush and knelt behind it. When the soldiers had gone by she stood up and removed her cloak and the blossoms turned blue in her honour. Also connected to the Christian faith is the story that rosemary will grow for 33 years, the length of Christ's life, and then die.

In Elizabethan days, the wedding couple wore or carried a sprig of rosemary as a sign of fidelity. Also bunches of rosemary were tied with coloured ribbon tipped with gold and given to guests at weddings to symbolize love and faithfulness.

Rosemary was burnt in sick chambers to freshen and purify the air. Branches were strewn in courts of law as a protection from gaol fever. During the Plague people used to wear it in neck pouches to sniff as they travelled, and in Victorian times it was carried in the hollow handles of walking sticks for the same reasons.

SPECIES

Rosmarinus officinalis
Rosemary
Evergreen hardy perennial. Ht and spread 1m (3ft). Pale blue flowers in early spring to early summer and then sometimes in early autumn. Needle-shaped dark green leaves are highly aromatic.

Rosmarinus officinalis var. albiflorus
White Rosemary
Evergreen hardy perennial. Ht and spread 80cm (32in). White flowers in early spring to early summer and then sometimes in early autumn. Needle-shaped dark green leaves are highly aromatic.

Rosmarinus officinalis angustissimus 'Corsican Blue'
Corsican Rosemary
Evergreen hardy perennial. Ht and spread 80cm (32in). Blue flowers in early spring to early summer and then sometimes again in early autumn. The needle shaped dark green leaves are highly aromatic. It is much bushier than the standard Rosemary and has a very pungent scent. It is lovely to cook with.

Rosmarinus officinalis 'Aureus'
Golden Rosemary
Evergreen hardy perennial. Ht 80cm (32in), spread 60cm (24in). It hardly ever flowers but if it does they are pale blue. The thin needle leaves are green splashed with gold. If you did not know better you would think the plant was suffering from a virus. It still looks very attractive.

Rosmarinus officinalis 'Benenden Blue'
Benenden Blue Rosemary
Evergreen hardy perennial. Ht and spread 80cm (32in). Dark blue flowers in early spring to early summer and then sometimes again in early autumn. Leaves are fine needles and fairly dense on the stem, good aroma.

Prostrate Rosemary *Rosmarinus officinalis Prostrate Group*

Miss Jessopp's Upright Rosemary *Rosmarinus officinalis 'Miss Jessopp's Upright'*

Rosmarinus officinalis 'Fota Blue'

Fota Blue Rosemary
Evergreen hardy perennial. Ht and spread 80cm (32in). Very attractive dark blue flowers in early spring to early summer and then sometimes again in early autumn. Very well spaced narrow needle-like dark green leaves, the plant has fairly prostrate habit.

Rosemary officinalis 'Majorca Pink'

Majorcan Pink Rosemary
Evergreen half-hardy perennial. Ht and spread 80cm (32in). Pink flowers in early spring to early summer and then sometimes again in early autumn. The needle-shaped dark green leaves are highly aromatic. This is a slightly prostrate form of Rosemary.

Rosmarinus officinalis 'Miss Jessopp's Upright'

Miss Jessopp's Upright Rosemary
Evergreen hardy perennial. Ht and spread 2m (6ft). Very pale blue flowers in early spring to early summer and then sometimes again in early autumn. This Rosemary has a very upright habit, making it ideal for hedges (see page 162). The leaves are dark green needles spaced closely together, making the plant very bushy.

Rosmarinus officinalis 'Primley Blue'

Primley Blue Rosemary
(Not Frimley which it has been incorrectly called for a few years.)
Evergreen hardy perennial. Ht and spread 80cm (32in). Blue flowers in early spring to early summer and then sometimes again in early autumn. The needle-shaped dark green leaves are highly aromatic. This is a good hardy bushy variety.

Rosmarinus officinalis Prostrate Group (lavandulaceus, repens)

Prostrate Rosemary
Evergreen hardy perennial. Ht 30cm (12in), spread 1m (3ft). Light blue flowers in early spring to early summer and then sometimes again in early autumn. The needle-shaped dark green leaves are highly aromatic. This is a great plant for trailing on a wall or bank.

Rosmarinus officinalis 'Roseus'

Pink Rosemary
Evergreen half-hardy perennial. Ht and spread 80cm (32in). Pink flowers in early spring to early summer and then sometimes again in early autumn. The needle-shaped dark green leaves are highly aromatic.

Rosmarinus officinalis 'Severn Sea'

Severn Seas Rosemary
Evergreen half-hardy perennial. Ht and spread 80cm (32in). Mid-blue flowers in early spring to early summer and then sometimes again in early autumn. The needle-shaped dark green leaves are highly aromatic. The whole plant has a slightly prostrate habit with arching branches.

Rosmarinus officinalis 'Sissinghurst Blue'

Sissinghurst Rosemary
Evergreen hardy perennial. Ht 1.5m (4½ft), spread 1m (3ft). Light blue flowers in early spring to early summer and then sometimes again in early autumn. The plant has an upright habit and grows very bushy. The needle-shaped dark green leaves are highly aromatic.

Rosmarinus officinalis 'Sudbury Blue'

Sudbury Blue Rosemary
Evergreen hardy perennial. Ht and spread 1m (3ft). Mid-blue flowers in early spring to early summer and then sometimes again in early autumn. Good hardy plant. The needle-shaped dark green leaves are highly aromatic.

I have some very old gardening books which make reference to a silver variegated rosemary, as does the RHS *Dictionary of Gardening* (1951) and I have even recently been asked if I grow it. I have yet to find it.

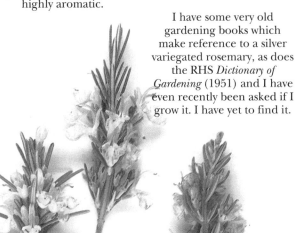

Left to right: **White Rosemary** *Rosmarinus officinalis var. albiflorus*, **Miss Jessopp's Upright Rosemary** *Rosmarinus officinalis 'Miss Jessopp's Upright'*, **Pink Rosemary** *Rosmarinus officinalis 'Roseus'*

CULTIVATION

Propagation
Seed
Rosemary officinalis can, with care, be grown from seed. It needs a bottom heat of 27-32°C (80-90°F) to be successful. Sow in the spring in prepared seed or plug trays, using the bark, peat, grit compost and cover with Perlite. Having got it to germinate be careful not to over-water the seedlings as they are prone to damping off. Harden the young plant off slowly in summer and pot up. Keep it in a pot for the first winter, and plant out the following spring into the required position at a distance if 60-90cm (2-3 ft) apart.

Cuttings
This is a more reliable method of propagation and ensures that you achieve the variety you require.

Softwood: Take these in spring off the new growth. Cut lengths of about 15cm (6in) long. Use the bark, grit, peat mix of compost.

Semi-hardwood: Take these in summer from the non-flowering shoots, using the same compost as for softwood cuttings.

Layering
Rosemary lends itself to layering especially as the branches of several varieties hang down. Layer established branches in summer.

Pests and Diseases
Being an aromatic plant, rosemary really does not suffer too much from pest and disease.

Maintenance
Spring: Trim after flowering. Sow seeds of **Rosemary officinalis**. Take softwood cuttings.
Summer: Feed container plants. Take semi-hardwood cuttings. Layer plants.
Autumn: Protect young tender plants.
Winter: Put a mulch, or straw, or agricultural fleece around all plants.

Garden Cultivation
Rosemary requires a well-drained soil in a sheltered sunny position. It is frost hardy but in cold areas it prefers to grow against a south or south-west facing wall. If the plant is young it is worth giving some added protection in winter. If trimming is necessary cut back only when the frosts are over; if possible leave it until after the spring flowering. Sometimes rosemary looks a bit scorched after frosts, in which case it is worth cutting the damaged plants to healthy wood in spring. Straggly old plants may also be cut back hard at the same time. Never cut back plants in the autumn or if there is any chance of frost, as the plant will be damaged or even killed. On average, despite the story about rosemary growing for 33 years, it is best to replace bushes every 5 to 6 years.

Harvest
As rosemary is evergreen, you can pick fresh leaves all year round as long as you are not greedy. If you need large quantities then harvest in summer and either dry the leaves or make an oil or vinegar.

COMPANION PLANTING

If planted near carrot it repels carrot fly. It is also said to be generally beneficial to sage.

Golden Rosemary *Rosmarinus officinalis 'Aureus'*

CONTAINER GROWING

Rosemary does well in pots and is the preferred way to grow it in cold districts. The prostrate and less hardy varieties look very attractive and benefit from the extra protection offered by a container. Use the bark, grit, peat mix and make sure the compost is very well drained. Do not over-water, and feed only after flowering.

HEDGES
Rosemary certainly makes an effective hedge; it looks pretty in flower, smells marvellous and is evergreen. In fact it has everything going for it if you have the right soil conditions which, more importantly than ever, must be well drained and carry a bias towards lime. The best varieties for hedges are Primley Blue and Miss Jessopp's. Both are upright, hardy and bushy. Primley Blue has a darker blue flower and I think is slightly prettier. Planting distance 45cm (18in) apart. Again, if you need eventually to trim the hedge, do it after the spring flowering.

CULINARY

This is one of the most useful of culinary herbs, combining with meat, especially lamb, casseroles, tomato sauces, baked fish, rice, salads, egg dishes, apples, summer wine cups, cordials, vinegars and oils.

Vegetarian Goulash
Serves 4

2 tablespoons rosemary olive oil
2 medium onions, sliced
1 dessertspoon wholemeal flour
1 tablespoon paprika
275ml (10fl oz) hot water mixed
  with 1 teaspoon tomato purée
400gm (14oz) tin Italian
  tomatoes
2 sprigs 10cm (4in) long
  Rosemary
225g (8oz) cauliflower sprigs
225g (8oz) new carrots, washed
  and cut into chunks
225g (8oz) new potatoes,
  washed and cut into halves
½ green pepper, de-seeded and
  chopped
150ml (5fl oz) soured cream or
  Greek yoghurt
Salt and freshly milled black
  pepper

Vegetarian Goulash

Heat the rosemary oil in a flameproof casserole, fry the onion until soft, then stir in the ¾ of the paprika. Cook for 2 minutes. Stir in the water, tomatoes and sprigs of rosemary. Bring to the boil stirring all the time. Add all the vegetables and the seasonings. Cover and bake in the pre-heated oven (190°C, 375°F, Gas Mark 5) for 30-40 minutes. Remove from oven, carefully take out the rosemary sprigs and stir in the soured cream or yoghurt, plus the remaining paprika. Serve with fresh pasta and/or garlic bread.

OTHER USES

Put rosemary twigs on the barbecue; they give off a delicious aroma. If you have a wood burning stove, a few twigs thrown onto it makes the house smell lovely.

Rosemary is used in many herbal shampoos and the plant has a long reputation as a hair tonic. Use an infusion in the final rinse of a hair wash, especially if you have dark hair, as it will make it shine. (Use chamomile for fair hair.)

Rosemary infusion

MEDICINAL

Like many other essential oils, rosemary oil has anti-bacterial and anti-fungal properties, and it helps poor circulation if rubbed into the effected joints.

The oil may be used externally as an insect repellent. It also makes an excellent remedy for headaches if applied directly to the head.

Rosemary tea makes a good mouthwash for halitosis and is also a good antiseptic gargle. Drunk in small amounts it reduces flatulence and stimulates the smooth muscle of the digestive tract and gall

bladder and increases the flow of bile. Put a teaspoon of chopped leaves into a cup and pour on boiling water; cover and leave it to stand for 5 minutes.

An antiseptic solution of rosemary can be added to the bath to promote heathy skin. Boil a handful in 475ml (16fl oz) of water for 10 minutes.

WARNING

The oil should not be used internally. Also, extremely large doses of the leaf are toxic, possibly causing abortion, convulsions and, very rarely, death.

'How can a man grow old who has sage in his garden?'
Ancient Proverb

Salvia

SAGE

From the family Labiatae

This large family of over 750 species is widely distributed throughout the world. It consists of annuals, biennials and perennials, herbs, sub-shrubs and shrubs of various habits. It is an important horticultural group. I have concentrated on the medicinal, culinary and a special aromatic species.

The name Salvia is derived from the Latin 'salveo' meaning I save or heal, because some species have been highly regarded medicinally.

The Greeks used it to heal ulcers, consumption, and snake bites. The Romans considered it a sacred herb to be gathered with ceremony. A special knife was used, not made of iron because sage reacts with iron salts. The sage gatherer had to wear clean clothes, have clean feet and make a sacrifice of food before the ceremony could begin. Sage was held to be good for the brain, the senses and memory. It also made a good gargle and mouthwash and was used as a toothpaste.

There are many stories about why the Chinese valued it so highly, and in the 17th century Dutch merchants found that the Chinese would trade 3 chests of China tea for 1 of sage leaves.

Above: **Sage** *Salvia officinalis*

Right: **Purple Sage** *Salvia officinalis Purpurascens Group*

SPECIES

I have only chosen a very few species to illustrate, they are the main ones used in cooking and medicine – with one exception, with which I begin.

Salvia elegans 'Scarlet Pineapple' (rutilans)
Pineapple Sage
Half-hardy perennial. Ht 90cm (3ft), spread 60cm (2ft). Striking red flowers, mid- to late summer. The leaves are green with a slight red tinge to the edges and have a glorious pineapple scent. This sage is sub-tropical and must be protected from frost during the winter. In temperate climates it is basically a house plant and if kept on a sunny windowsill can be used throughout the year. It can only be grown from cuttings. This is an odd sage to cook with, it does not taste as well as it smells. It is fairly good combined with apricots as a stuffing for pork, otherwise my culinary experiments with it have not met with great success.

Salvia lavandulifolia
Narrowed-Leaved Sage
Also known as Spanish Sage. Hardy evergreen perennial. Ht and spread 45cm (18in). Attractive blue flowers in summer. The leaves are green with a texture, small, thin, and oval in shape and highly aromatic. This is an excellent sage to cook with, very pungent. It also makes a good tea. Can only be grown from cuttings.

Salvia officinalis
Sage
Also known as Common Sage, Garden Sage, Broad Leaved Sage, and Sawge. Hardy evergreen perennial. Ht and spread 60cm (2ft). Mauve/blue flowers in summer. The leaves are green with a texture, thin and oval in shape and highly aromatic. This is the best known sage for culinary use. Can be easily grown from seed. There is also a white flowering sage **Salvia officinalis 'Albiflora'**, which is quite rare.

Salvia officinalis Broad-leaved (latifolia)
Broad-Leaved Sage
Hardy evergreen perennial. Ht and spread 60cm (2ft). Very rarely flowers in cool climates, if it does they are blue/mauve in colour. The leaves are green with a texture, larger than the ordinary sage, with an oval shape and highly aromatic. Good for cooking. Can only be grown from cuttings.

Salvia officinalis icterina
Gold Sage
Hardy evergreen perennial. Ht 45cm (18in), spread 75cm (30in). Very rarely flowers in cool climates, if it does they are blue/mauve in colour. The leaves are green/gold variegated with a texture, small and oval in shape and aromatic. A mild flavour but equally good to cook with. Can only be grown from cuttings.

Clary Sage *Salvia sclarea*

Salvia sclarea
Clary Sage

Also known as Muscatel Sage.
Hardy biennial. Ht 60-90cm (2-3ft), spread 45cm (18in). Colourful flower bracts – blue/purple/lilac with a whitish base in summer. Leaves are often 20-23cm (8-9in) long, soft green in colour and slightly wrinkled. Easily grown from seed. There is another variety, **Salvia var. turkestanica**, with white flowers tinged with pink.

Salvia officinalis Purpurascens Group
Purple/Red Sage

Hardy evergreen perennial. Ht and spread 70cm (28in). Mauve/blue flowers in summer. The leaves are purple with a texture, a thin oval shape and aromatic. 2 points to think about.
If you clip it in the spring, it develops new leaves and looks really good but flowers only a small amount. If you do not clip it and allow it to flower it goes woody. If you then cut it back it does not produce new growth until the spring, so can look a bit bare. So what to do? There is also a variegated form of this purple sage **Salvia officinalis 'Purpurascens Variegata'**. Both of these can only be grown from cuttings.

Salvia officinalis 'Tricolor'
Tricolor Sage

Half-hardy evergreen perennial. Ht and spread 40cm (16in). Attractive blue flowers in summer. The leaves are green with pink, white and purple variegation, with a texture. They are small, thin, and oval in shape and highly aromatic. It has a mild flavour, so can be used in cooking. Can only be grown from cuttings.

CULTIVATION

Propagation
Seed

Common and clary sage grow successfully in the spring from seed sown into prepared seed or plug trays and covered with Perlite. The seeds are a good size. If starting off under protection in early spring, warmth is of benefit – temperatures of 15-21°C (60-70°F). Germination takes 2-3 weeks. Pot up or plant out when the frosts are over at a distance of 45-60cm (18-24in) apart.

Cuttings

This is a good method for all variegated species and the ones that do not set seed in cooler climates. Use the bark, peat mix of compost. *Softwood*: Take these cuttings in late spring or early summer from the strong new growth. All forms take easily from cuttings; rooting is about 4 weeks in summer. *Layering*: If you have a well-established sage, or if it is becoming a bit woody, layer established branches in spring or autumn.

Pests and Diseases

Sage grown in the garden does not suffer over much from pests and disease. Sage grown in containers, especially pineapple sage, is prone to red spider mite. As soon as you see this pest, treat with a liquid horticultural soap as per the instructions.

Maintenance

Spring: Sow seeds. Trim if needed, and then take softwood cuttings.
Summer: Trim back after flowering.
Autumn: Protect all half-hardy sages, and first-year plants.
Winter: Protect plants if they are needed for fresh leaves.

Purple Sage *Salvia officinalis Purpurascens Group* and **Gold Sage** *Salvia officinalis icterina*

Garden Cultivation

Sage, although predominately a Mediterranean plant, is sufficiently hardy to withstand any ordinary winter without protection, as long as the soil is well drained and not acid, and the site is as warm and dry as possible. The flavour of the leaf can vary as to how rich, damp, etc, the soil is. If wishing to sow seed outside, wait until there is no threat of frost and sow direct into prepared ground, spacing the seeds 23cm (9in) apart. After germination thin to 45cm (18in) apart. For the first winter cover the young plants with agricultural fleece or a mulch.
To keep the plants bushy prune in the spring to encourage young shoots for strong flavour, and also after flowering in late summer. Mature plants can be pruned hard in the spring after some cuttings have been taken as insurance. Never prune in the autumn as this can kill the plant. As sage is prone to becoming woody, replace the plant every 4-5 years.

Sage Bianco *Salvia blancoana* **has a silvery leaf and prostrate habit**

Harvest

Since sage is an evergreen plant, the leaves can be used fresh any time of the year. In Mediterranean-type climates, including the southern states of America, the leaves can be harvested during the winter months. In cooler climates this is also possible if you cover a chosen bush with agricultural fleece as this will keep the leaves in better condition. They dry well, but care should be taken to keep their green colour. Because this herb is frequently seen in its dried condition people presume it is easy to dry. But beware, although other herbs may lose some of their aroma or qualities if badly dried or handled, sage seems to pick up a musty scent and a flavour really horrible to taste – better to grow it in your garden to use fresh.

CONTAINER GROWING

All sages grow happily in containers. Pineapple sage is an obvious one as it is tender, but a better reason is that if it is at hand one will rub the leaves and smell that marvellous pineapple scent. Use the bark, grit, peat mix of compost for all varieties, feed the plants after flowering, and do not over-water.

COMPANION PLANTING

Sage planted with cabbages is said to repel cabbage white butterflies. Planted next to vines it is generally beneficial.

OTHER USES

The dried leaves, especially those of pineapple sage, are good added to potpourris.

Broad-Leaved Sage *Salvia officinalis broad-leaved*

MEDICINAL

For centuries, sage has been esteemed for its healing powers. It is a first rate remedy as a hot infusion for colds. Sage tea combined with a little cider vinegar makes a gargle which is excellent for sore throats, laryngitis and tonsillitis. *It is also beneficial for infected gums and mouth ulcers.*

The essential oil, known as Sage Clary or Muscatel Oil, is obtained by steamed distillation of the fresh or partially dried flower stems *and leaves. It is used in herbal medicine but more widely in toilet waters, perfumes and soap, and to flavour wine, vermouth and liqueurs.*

Left: **Tricolor Sage** *Salvia officinalis 'Tricolor'*

CULINARY

This powerful healing plant is also a strong culinary herb, although it has been misused and misjudged in the culinary world. Used with discretion it adds a lovely flavour, aids digestion of fatty food, and being an antiseptic it kills off any bugs in the meat as it cooks. It has long been used with sausages because of its preservative qualities. It also makes a delicious herb jelly, or oil or vinegar. But I like using small amounts fresh. The original form of the following recipe comes from a vegetarian friend of mine. I fell in love with it and have subsequently adapted it to include some other herbs.

Hazelnut and Mushroom Roast
Serves 4

A little sage oil
Long grain brown rice (measured to the 150ml (5fl oz) mark on a glass measuring jug)
275ml (10fl oz) boiling water
1 teaspoon salt
1 large onion, peeled and chopped
110g (4oz) mushrooms, wiped and chopped
2 medium carrots, pared and roughly grated
½ teaspoon coriander seed
1 tablespoon soy sauce
110g (4oz) wholemeal breadcrumbs
175g (6oz) ground hazelnuts
1 teaspoon chopped sage leaves
1 teaspoon chopped lovage leaves
Sunflower seeds for decoration
A 900g (2lb) loaf tin, lined with greaseproof paper

Pre-heat the oven (180°C 350°F, Gas Mark 4).

Heat 1 dessertspoon of sage oil in a small saucepan, toss the rice in it to give it a coating of oil, add boiling water straight from the kettle and the teaspoon of salt. Stir, and let the rice cook slowly for roughly 40 minutes or until the liquid has been absorbed.

While the rice is cooking, heat 1 tablespoon of sage oil in a medium sized frying-pan, add the onions, mushrooms, carrots, the ground coriander seed and soy sauce. Mix them together and let them cook for about 10 minutes.

Combine the cooked brown rice, breadcrumbs, hazelnuts, sage and lovage; mix with the vegetables and place the complete mixture in the prepared loaf tin. Scatter the sunflower seeds on top and bake in the oven

Hazelnut and mushroom roast, a delicious dish for vegetarians

for 45 minutes. Leave to cool slightly in the tin. Slice and serve with a home-made tomato sauce and a green salad.

WARNING

Extended or excessive use of sage can cause symptoms of poisoning. Although the herb seems safe and common, it you drink the tea for more than a week or two at a time, its strong antiseptic properties can cause potentially toxic effects.

Satureja (Satureia)

SAVORY

From the family Labiatae.

avory is a native of southern Europe and North Africa, especially around the Mediterranean. It grows in well-drained soils and has adapted worldwide to similar climatic conditions. Savory has been employed in food flavouring for over 2,000 year. Romans added it to sauces and vinegars, which they used liberally as flavouring. The Ancient Egyptians on the other hand used it in love potions. The Romans also included it in their wagon train to northern Europe, where it became an invaluable disinfectant strewing herb. It was also used to relieve tired eyes, for ringing in the ears, indigestion, wasp and bee stings, and for other shocks to the system.

Winter Savory *Satureja montana*

SPECIES

Summer Savory
Satureja hortensis

Satureja hortensis
Summer Savory
Also known as Bean Herb. Half-hardy annual. Ht 20-30cm (8-12in), spread 15cm (6in). Small white/mauve flowers in summer. Aromatic leaves, oblong, pointed, and green. A favourite on the Continent and in America, where it is known as the bean herb. It has become widely used in bean dishes as it helps prevent flatulence.

Satureja coerulea
Purple-Flowered Savory
Semi-evergreen hardy perennial. Ht 30cm (12in), spread 20cm (8in). Small purple flowers in summer. The leaves are darkish green, linear and very aromatic.

Satureja montana
Winter Savory
Also known as Mountain Savory.
Semi-evergreen hardy perennial. Ht 30cm (12in), spread 20cm (8in). Small white/pink flowers in summer. The leaves are dark green, linear and very aromatic.

Satureja spicigera
Creeping Savory
Perennial. Ht 8cm (3in), spread 30cm (12in). Masses of small white flowers in summer. The leaves are lime greenish and linear. This is a most attractive plant and is often mistaken for thyme or even heather.

CULTIVATION

Propagation
Seed
Only summer and winter savory can be grown from seed, which is tiny, so it is best to sow into prepared seed trays under protection in the early spring, using the cardboard method. The seeds should not be covered as they need light to germinate. Germination takes about 10-15 days – no need to use bottom heat. When the seedlings are large enough, and after a period of hardening off (making quite sure that the frosts have finished), they can be planted out into a prepared site in the garden, 15cm (6in) apart.

Cuttings
Creeping, purple-flowered and winter savory can all be grown from softwood cuttings in spring, using a bark, peat, grit compost. When these have rooted they should be planted out – 30cm (12in) apart for creeping savory, 15cm (6in) apart for the others.

Division
Creeping savory can be divided, as each section has its own root system similar to creeping thymes. Dig up an established plant in the spring after the frosts have finished and divide into as many segments as you require. Minimum size is only dependent on each having a root system and how long you are prepared to wait for new plants to become established. Replant in a prepared site.

Pests and Diseases

Being an aromatic plant savory is, in the main, free from pests and disease.

Maintenance

Spring: Sow seed. Take softwood cuttings. Divide established plants.
Summer: Keep picking and do not allow summer savory to flower, if you want to maintain its flavour.
Autumn: Protect from prolonged frosts.
Winter: Protect.

Garden Cultivation

All the above mentioned savories like full sun and a poor, well-drained soil. Plant summer savory in the garden in a warm sheltered spot and keep picking the leaves to stop it getting leggy. Do not feed with liquid fertilizer, otherwise the plant will keel over.

Winter savory can make a good edging plant and is very pretty in the summer, although it can look a bit sparse in the winter months. Again, trim it from time to time to maintain shape and promote new growth. Creeping savory does not like cold wet winters, or for that matter clay soil, so on this nursery I grow it in a pot (see below). If, however, you wish to grow it in your garden, plant it in a sunny rockery or a well-drained, sheltered corner.

Harvest

For fresh use, pick leaves as required. For drying, pick those of summer savory before it flowers. They dry easily.

CONTAINER GROWING

All savories can be grown in containers, and if your garden suffers from prolonged cold wet winters

Savory is an important constituent of salami

it may be the only way you can grow this delightful plant successfully. Use the bark, peat, grit mix of compost. Pick the plants continuously to maintain shape, especially the summer savory which can get straggly. If you are picking the plants a lot they may benefit from a feed of liquid fertilizer, but keep this to a minimum as they get over eager when fed.

Summer savory, being an annual, dies in winter, creeping savory dies back, the winter savory is a partial evergreen. So, the latter 2 will need protection in winter. Place them in a cool greenhouse or conservatory. If the container cannot be moved, wrap it up in paper or agricultural fleece. Keep watering to the absolute minimum.

MEDICINAL

Summer savory is the plant credited with medicinal virtues and is said to alleviate the pain of bee stings if rubbed on the affected spot. Infuse as a tea to stimulate appetite and to ease indigestion and flatulence. It is also considered a stimulant and was once in demand as an aphrodisiac.

Winter savory is also used medicinally but is inferior.

CULINARY

The two savories used in cooking are winter and summer savory. The other varieties are edible but their flavour is inferior. Summer and winter savory combine well with vegetables, pulses and rich meats. These herbs stimulate the appetite and aid digestion. The flavour is hot and peppery, and so should be added sparingly in salads.

Summer Savory can replace both salt and pepper and is a great help to those on a salt free diet. It is a pungent herb and until one is familiar with its strength it should be used carefully. Summer savory also makes a good vinegar and oil. The oil is used commercially as a flavouring, as is the leaf, which is an important constituent of salami.

The flavour of winter savory is both coarser and stronger, its advantage is that it provides fresh leaves into early winter.

Beans with Garlic and Savory
Serves 3-4

200g (7oz) dried haricot beans
1 Spanish onion
1 carrot, scrubbed and roughly sliced
1 stick celery
1 clove garlic
3 tablespoons olive oil
1 tablespoon white wine vinegar
2 tablespoons chopped summer savory
2 tablespoons chopped French parsley

Soak the beans in cold water overnight or for at least 3-4 hours. Drain them and put them in a saucepan with plenty of water. Bring to the boil slowly. Add half the peeled onion, the carrot and celery, and cook until tender. As soon as the beans are soft, drain and discard the vegetables. Mix the oil, vinegar and crushed garlic. While the beans are still hot, stir in the remaining half onion (thinly sliced), the chopped herbs, and pour over the oil and vinegar dressing. Serve soon after cooling. Do not chill.

Beans with garlic and savory

Glycyrrhiza glabra

LIQUORICE

**Also known as Licorice, Sweet Licorice and Sweetwood.
From the family Leguminosae.**

This plant, which is a native of the Mediterranean region, is commercially grown throughout the temperate zones of the world and extensively cultivated in Russia, Iran, Spain and India. It has been used medicinally for 3,000 years and was recorded on Assyrian tablets and Egyptian papyri. The Latin name *Glycyrrhiza* comes from 'glykys' meaning sweet, and 'rhiza' root.

It was first introduced to England by Dominican friars in the 16th century and became an important crop. The whole of the huge cobbled courtyard of medieval Pontefract Castle was covered by top soil to grow liquorice. It is sad that Pontefract cakes are made from imported liquorice today.

Liquorice sticks

SPECIES

Glycyrrhiza glabra
Liquorice
Hardy perennial. Ht 1.2m (4ft), spread 1m (3ft). Pea-like, purple/blue and white flowers borne in short spikes on erect stems in late summer. Large greenish leaves divided into oval leaflets.

CULTIVATION

Propagation
Seed
The seedlings often damp off. In cooler climates the seed tends not to be viable. Root division is much easier.

Division
Divide when the plant is dormant, making sure the root has 1 or more buds. Place into pots half filled with compost. Cover with compost. Water well and leave in a warm place until shoots appear. Harden off, then plant out in early spring or autumn. If the latter, winter in a cold greenhouse or cold frame.

Pests and Diseases
Largely pest and disease free.

Maintenance
Spring: Divide established plants.
Summer: Do nothing.
Autumn: Divide established plants if necessary.
Winter: In very cold winters protect first year plants.

Garden Cultivation
Liquorice needs a rich, deep, well-cultivated soil.
Plant pieces of the root, each with a bud, directly into a prepared site 15cm (6in) deep and 1m (3ft) apart in early spring or in autumn during the dormant season if the ground is workable and not frosty.
Liquorice does best in long, hot summers, but will need extra watering if your soil is very free draining.

Harvest
Harvest roots for drying in early winter from established 3 or 4 year old plants.

CONTAINER GROWING

Never displays as well as in the garden. Use a soil-based compost. Feed throughout the growing season and water until it dies back.

CULINARY

Liquorice is used as a flavouring in the making of Guinness and other beers.

MEDICINAL

The juice from the roots provides commercial liquorice. It is used either to mask the unpleasant flavour of other medicines or to provide its own soothing action on troublesome coughs. The dried root, stripped of its bitter bark, is recommended as a remedy for colds, sore throats and bronchial catarrh.
Liquorice is a gentle laxative and lowers stomach acid levels, so relieving heartburn. It has a remarkable power to heal stomach ulcers because it spreads a protective gel over the stomach wall and in addition it eases spasms of large intestine. It also increases the flow of bile and lowers blood cholesterol levels.

WARNING

Large doses of liquorice causes side effects, notably headaches, high blood pressure and water retention.